Jazzing Up Instruction

*An Integrated Curriculum for
Elementary Students*

Created by Kelly Spanoghe
Stories written by Bill Messenger

The Children's Guild
and
The Scarecrow Press, Inc.
Lanham, Maryland, and Oxford
2002

SCARECROW PRESS, INC.

Published in the United States of America
by Scarecrow Press, Inc.
A Member of the Rowman & Littlefield Publishing Group
4720 Boston Way, Lanham, Maryland 20706
www.scarecrowpress.com

PO Box 317
Oxford
OX2 9RU, UK

British Library Cataloguing in Publication Information Available

Library of Congress Cataloging-in-Publication Data Available

ISBN 1-931596-00-X (pbk. : alk. paper)

♾™ The paper used in this publication meets the minimum requirements of
American National Standard for Information Sciences—Permanence of
Paper for Printed Library Materials, ANSI/NISO Z39.48-1992.
Manufactured in the United States of America.

Table of Contents

The Research Behind *Jazzing Up Instruction:* Why It Helps Children Learn

Music is a universal language that has been recognized throughout history for its ability to entertain, communicate, educate, inspire, infuse customs, impart values and allow people to relate to one another. All of these are essential components for educational benefit. Music has a profound effect on a student's availability to the learning process, and therefore impacts the student's ability to achieve to his/her capability. Richard Riley, former Secretary of Education, reflects on the impact of the arts, "The ultimate challenge for American education is to place all children on pathways toward success in school and in life. Through engagement with the arts, young people can better begin lifelong journeys of developing their capabilities and contributing to the world around them. As researchers have confirmed, young people can be better prepared for the 21st century through quality learning experiences in, and through, the arts" (MUSICA Research Notes).

Music is an effective tool for learning. Evidence from brain research suggests that music plays an important role in brain development. Music stimulates and unifies brain function by incorporating three modalities; (1) auditory, (2) kinesthetic and (3) tactual. When the lyrics are present, then the visual modality is also engaged. Music can be considered a tool for learning in three categories: for arousal of attentional neurotransmitters, as a carrier of information through the melody or rhythm, and for priming the brain's neural pathway, resulting in clear thinking. The ability to activate and synchronize neural firing patterns that orchestrate and connect multiple brain sites correlates to greater learner engagement in the educational process. The activation of multiple brain sites results in higher brain functioning and more focused thinking. Integration of music into daily instruction not only increases the student's ability to focus attention, but it also enables them to utilize higher level thinking strategies.

Music is a powerful tool for emotional memory. The beat, melody and harmonies serve as carriers for the semantic content, which works to aid memory. Rhythmic patterns have a profound effect on the body and its emotional states. It can reduce mental fatigue, calm tension,focus thinking and stimulate creativity. Music evokes emotions in the listener that accelerates and enhances the ability of the learner to assess a situation and act in accordance. Emotions aroused through music activate procedural memory. The brain stores information if it is found to be useful, rhythmic or emotionally charged. Rhythmic data is stored in long term memory that can be combined with learning in various subject areas. Emotions drive attention; attention drives learning. Howard Gardner's theory on Multiple Intelligence reminds us that musical intelligence must be considered when tailoring education to the individual needs of the learner.

Research suggests that music facilitates the developing of skills necessary to be a successful reader. Phonemic awareness has been identified as the most potent predictor of success in learning to read. Phonemic awareness pertains to the ability to reflect on speech, detect phonemes and experiment with them to produce language. It is developed through engagement in rich language activities that encourage active exploration and manipulation of sound. Music provides a vehicle by which children can learn to discriminate and identify sounds. A close relationship exists between a child's control over sound and the ability to read. Educational research has determined a high correlation between pitch discrimination and reading skills. Music encourages children to produce speech sounds through singing. Repetition is an instructional strategy frequently used to develop reading skills and occurs naturally in music. Singing invites a repetition of lyrics and provides a normal manner for rehearsal of sound production. Reading activities that develop listening and expressive skills include musical components such as nursery rhymes, singing, chanting, listening and writing song lyrics. These language activities can be integrated into all curricular areas. Therefore, music forms a natural bridge to literacy and a valuable tool for developing reading skills.

A wide range of academic skills is impacted by music. Research also indicates that beneficial effects have been found in the areas of language development, thinking skills, problem-solving abilities, general intellectual achievement, self-esteem and positive attitudes toward school. Teachers concur that students demonstrate increased motivation, which fosters greater academic achievement and a positive school climate. Research conducted with various age groups (kindergarten through high school) emphasizes the importance of integrating music into the curriculum to develop thinking and behaviors needed to succeed in life.

The creation of song lyrics provides a powerful avenue for identification and use of emotional states for expression of feelings. This is because emotions are communicated through song lyrics and rhythm. Listening to various forms of music thereby increases emotional awareness and self understanding.

Integration of music into all curricular areas has proven to benefit students in a multitude of ways. Music experiences enrich the learning process, and introduce an element of fun, thus making learning more inherently interesting and motivating for students. Feelings are critical to the learning process and determine how long information will be retained. Learning is not real until the brain "feels" it. Therefore, learning without feelings is incomplete. Integrated music experiences provide excitement for learning, expands the instructional process while accommodating differences in learning styles and instills feelings into the instructional environment.

Review of educational research supports the assumption that a strong foundation in the arts builds creativity, concentration, problem solving, self-efficacy, coordination and self-discipline. These elements are essential components in the learning process and are embedded in the *Jazzing Up Instruction* curriculum.

References

Brown, Ron and Nancy. <u>Use Music To Teach!</u> (California: 1991).

Bryan, Sandra L. and Sprague, Marsha M. <u>Educating the Spirit for Beauty</u>. (Vol. 2, Number 4, December 1998/January 1999).

Chipongian, Lisa. <u>What is "Brain-Based Learning?"</u> (California, 1999).

Hanson, E. Simon, <u>A New Approach to Learning: The Theory of Multiple Intelligences.</u> (California, 1999).

Jensen, Eric. <u>Arts with the Brain in Mind</u> (Virginia: ASCD, 2001).

Jensen, Eric, <u>Brain Compatible Strategies</u> (San Diego: ASCD, 1997).

Jensen, Eric, <u>Teaching with the Brain in Mind</u> (San Diego: ASCD, 1998).

Musselwhite, Caroline Ramsey. <u>Singing to learn: Using music to jump-start language, literacy and life!</u>

Sousa, David A. <u>How the Brain Learns</u> (Virginia: National Association of Secondary School Principals, 1995).

Weinberger, N.M. <u>The Impact of the Arts on Learning</u>. (Volume VII, Issue 2, Spring, 2000).

Yopp, Hallie Kay. <u>Building a Powerful Reading Program.</u>

Teacher Workbook Overview

The *Jazzing Up Instruction* teacher workbook was developed to assist teachers with incorporating music into classroom instruction. Music makes learning fun, which fosters student engagement. When students become excited about learning, they feel a sense of accomplishment and will achieve to their capability. It increases a sense of inclusion and encourages collaboration among students. Much like a jazz concert, when students participate in cooperative learning activities, it enables them to bridge concepts, synthesize information and increase their self-esteem.

The *Jazzing Up Instruction* teacher workbook incorporates flexibility in its implementation. It is designed for use with grades one through five. However, it can be adapted for any grade with some adjustments to lesson objectives, instructional delivery techniques, and outcome measures. The workbook can be utilized as an entire unit of study, as a single lesson or broken into subject areas. Teachers are encouraged to utilize the curriculum in a fashion that meets the learning profile of the students and in accordance with their standard curriculum. It is not how the curriculum is incorporated, but rather that music becomes an important component in the learning process.

The workbook design is based on an integrated curriculum format. This approach assists students in understanding the interconnectedness between concepts, utilizes a real life problem-oriented approach and focuses on conceptualization rather than memorization. When students experience learning they remember it and can apply it to future lessons. Just as with music, until you "feel" the music it isn't real. Research on brain functions concurs with this process of "feeling" the learning experience.

An overview is provided for each story contained in the teacher workbook. Teachers who are unfamiliar with the integrated curriculum format, or for the novice teacher, the overview describes the proposed grade level, the instructional objectives, how concepts are integrated and ways to bridge concepts/subject matter. The overview will assist teachers in creatively implementing the curriculum and motivate them to engage students in academic activities that will inspire them to succeed.

The *Jazzing Up Instruction* workbook contains ten stories and supplemental materials. Each story is accompanied by an integrated curriculum graphic organizer that serves as a unifying theme among curricular concepts. This storyline provides a central theme, or main idea, upon which the curriculum is integrated. Each graphic organizer outlines concept connections for the subjects: reading, social skills, math, social studies, language arts, music, art, physical education, science and health. It is important to recognize the cultural arts as a means of extending classroom learning opportunities and enhancing concept comprehension and retention.

The stories included in the workbook incorporate various aspects of the jazz movement. Historical perspectives on various periods of time, chronicles of famous jazz musicians, the songwriting process, and how music/records are produced are some of the topics found in the stories. The stories act as a springboard for countless learning opportunities.

Vocabulary lists are included to assist students with comprehension. Much of the vocabulary will be new to students as it pertains to music. Although the vocabulary is difficult for young readers, they will enjoy being able to read "big" words. To encourage age retention and usage, teachers can display the new vocabulary words on walls, personal dictionaries and encourage them in other aspects of teaching.

Comprehension questions are also provided for each story. They are developmentally based and encourage students to apply their learning rather than restate the information. This will assist students with reading for comprehension and strengthen their ability to utilize higher level thinking skills. Comprehension questions can be reviewed prior to reading the story. This provides a purpose for learning and will assist students who may have comprehension difficulties or as a follow-up after they have read the story to check their comprehension. For younger readers the stories should be read aloud, providing periodic comprehension checks.

Supplemental worksheets are included in the curriculum for each story to reinforce concept development. Many of the worksheets correspond to the story content and contain a musical element. They can be used as independent assignments, homework, or credit to best fit the student's learning needs.

The Jazzing Up Instruction CD contains ten songs that reinforce the development of prosocial behaviors. The CD complements the workbook by demonstrating how perseverance and hard work result in positive outcomes. The music evokes emotions, motivates the learner, stimulates language development and creates lasting memories. Teachers can use the CD to create an exciting learning environment full of emotion and rich language.

Another component of the *Jazzing Up Instruction* curriculum is the inclusion of character education. Given the attention that character education has received in society due to the aberrant behaviors of our youth, this curriculum incorporates the development of social skills at various developmental levels. Students will be encouraged to explore feeling states, recognize body language, demonstrate respect towards others, increase self-esteem, and improve their pragmatic language skills. The use of role-playing and drama provides opportunities for students to practice appropriate, socially acceptable behaviors.

Implementation of the *Jazzing Up Instruction* curriculum expands the academic and social/emotional curriculum continuum in a way that will energize and enthuse the learner. Integration of music into classroom instruction provides a creative venue for teachers to inspire young minds and achieve academic excellence. So . . . Jazz it up!

Your feedback is appreciated in knowing how the workbook lessons are working. Please feel free to contact me at 410-636-7255 or email spanoghe@childrensguild.org.

Kelly Spanoghe, Ed.S.
Director of Educational Service
The Children's Guild

Overview
"How Come You Do Me"

This story describes the production of records and acoustical recordings. The integrated curriculum is based on <u>first</u> grade curricular concepts.*

Themes:
The themes of this story center on these concepts:
- Consonant blends
- Sound vibrations
- Goods and services
- Money concepts
- Production of phonographs and records

Integration of Themes:
The following connections can be made between the curricular concepts and the story line:

- The story focuses on treating others, as you wish to be treated, exemplifying the give and take exchange. This relates to the purchase of goods and services. Students become aware of the concepts of supply and demand, natural resources and how to make a purchase. These themes reinforce how the concept of money is used to represent goods and services, the ability to compare and contrast and an understanding of communities.

- Another theme throughout the story is the production of records and the comparison with how music products are made today. Through the study of vibrations in science, students begin to broaden their understanding of how sound is produced and then recorded. Students can produce their own records and try out these concepts first hand.

* The teacher should read the story and then tell it to the class. Next, teach the vocabulary of the story and tell the story again to the class, periodically checking for comprehension.

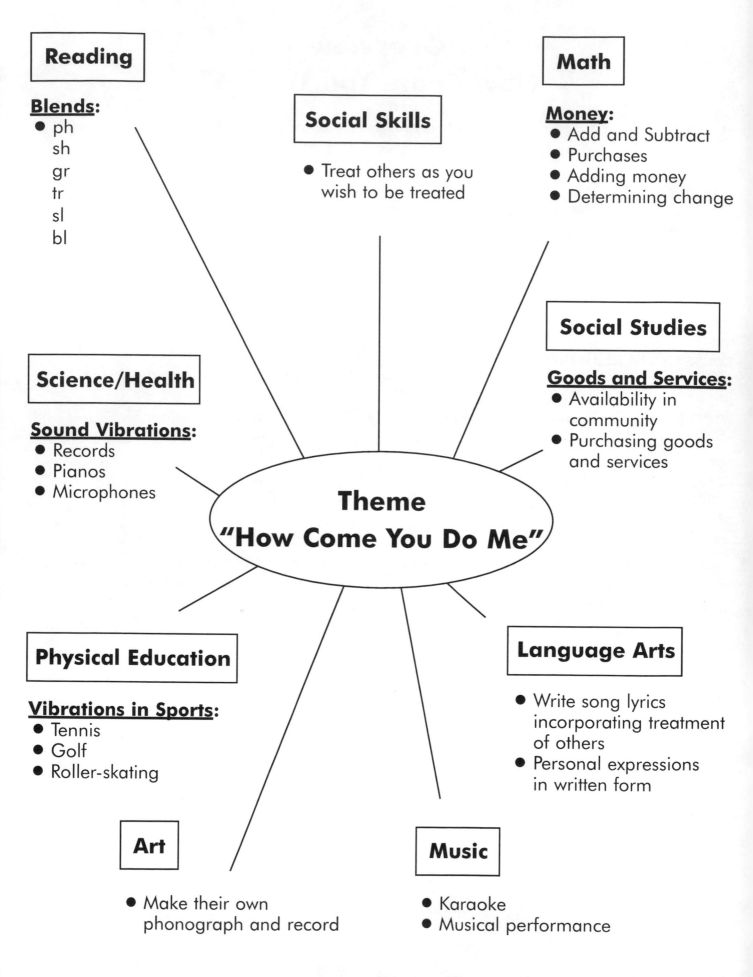

Reading

Blends:
- ph
  sh
  gr
  tr
  sl
  bl

Social Skills

- Treat others as you wish to be treated

Math

Money:
- Add and Subtract
- Purchases
- Adding money
- Determining change

Social Studies

Goods and Services:
- Availability in community
- Purchasing goods and services

Science/Health

Sound Vibrations:
- Records
- Pianos
- Microphones

Theme
"How Come You Do Me"

Physical Education

Vibrations in Sports:
- Tennis
- Golf
- Roller-skating

Language Arts

- Write song lyrics incorporating treatment of others
- Personal expressions in written form

Art

- Make their own phonograph and record

Music

- Karaoke
- Musical performance

12

"How Come You Do Me"

This song was written in 1924 by Gene Austin, a man who, four years later, would record the first million selling vocal recording - called "My Blue Heaven." At this time there were no million selling records because sheet music sold better than records. Many families owned pianos, but fewer families owned phonographs. The sound of phonograph records in 1924 was thin and scratchy, unlike the sound of CDs today.

Records in 1924 were "acoustically" recorded, not electrically recorded. To record electrically, a microphone was needed. However, the microphone wasn't invented until the end of 1924. (Because there were no microphones, jazz and blues singers had to sing very loudly to be heard above the bands. For this reason, these singers were often called "shouters").

Acoustical recording worked by laying a warm wax disc on a turntable. (The turntable made the disc rotate, clockwise, not by electricity, but by a spring inside the turntable. Wound by hand, the spring was released to make the turntable go around).

Suspended above the disc was a very large cardboard cone. Attached to the slender bottom of the cone was a sharp needle which cut a groove in the soft wax as the disc rotated. The singer sang into the wide part of the cardboard cone. The sound from her voice traveled down the cone to the needle which vibrated in sympathy with the voice as it cut the groove in the wax disc. The wax disc cooled and hardened and another less sharp needle was set on the disc which rotated again. This time the needle carried the sound up from the record groove, through the cardboard cone, out through the wide opening at the top, and into the listener's ear. That, basically, is all there was to acoustical recording.

This method of recording didn't always work too well. When singing, if the person backed away from the opening of the cone, their voice became very soft. If they accidentally moved to one side a little, they couldn't be heard at all. Since the needle wasn't sensitive to slow vibrations, often the string bass couldn't be heard at all.

Today, these acoustical recordings are all we know about the sound of early jazz. When listening to one of them, keep in mind that the live performance contained a lot more than could be heard. The difference between 1924 and 2001 can be heard in the CD which accompanies this book. It almost sounds like a live performance.

Song Lyrics
"How Come You Do Me"

(A)   How come you do me like you Do Do Do
          How come you do me like you Do

(A)   How come you do me like you Do Do Do
          How come you do me like you Do

(B)   Do me right or else let me be
          Cause you can be just as nice as me

(A)   How come you do me like you Do Do Do
          How come you do me like you Do

Comprehension
"How Come You Do Me"

1. How is the music in 2001 different from the music of 1924?

2. Why were there no million selling records in 1924?

3. Explain why recording music changed from acoustical to electrical.

4. What impact has recorded music had on our society?

Vocabulary
"How Come You Do Me"

Directions: Define the following words.

1. phonograph -

2. microphone -

3. groove -

4. traveled -

5. slender -

6. shout -

7. acoustical -

8. sheet -

Writing Song Lyrics
"How Come You Do Me"

Directions:

Write your own song lyrics. Create the second line of the song and share it with the class.

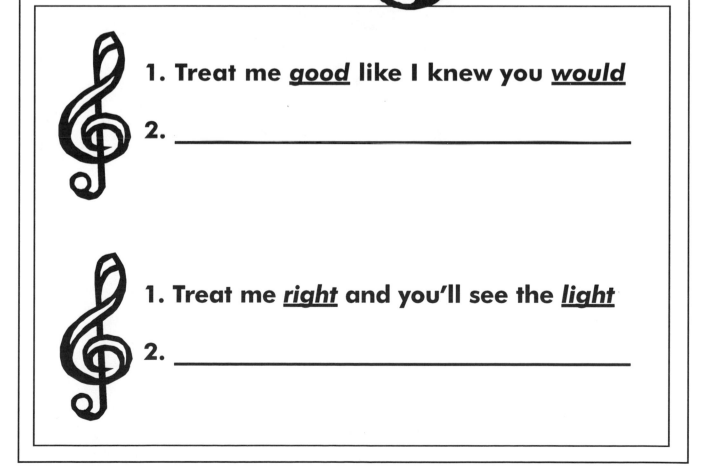

1. Treat me _good_ like I knew you _would_

2. _____

1. Treat me _right_ and you'll see the _light_

2. _____

Directions: 1. Cut out the <u>circle</u> below. Cut along the dotted line.

2. When finished, proceed to the following page.

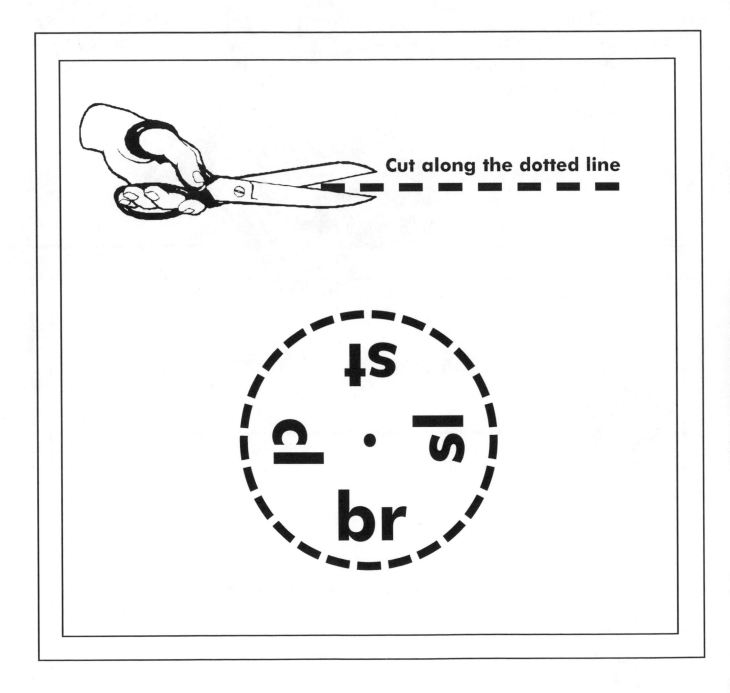

Cut along the dotted line

<u>Directions:</u> 1. **PLACE** the circle on **<u>TOP</u>** of the brown box below.

2. **TACK** the <u>center</u> of the circle to the brown box using a brass tack.

3. **When finished, the circle should turn.**

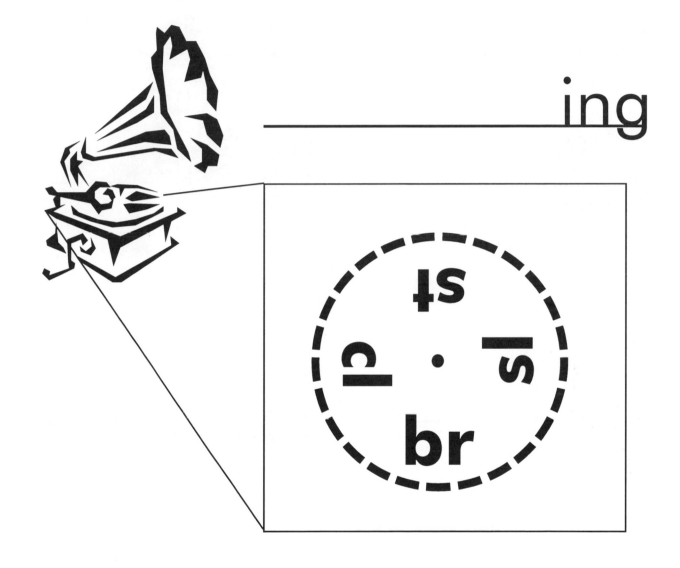

_____ing

| **<u>Step 2:</u>** Turn the record above to make <u>four</u> new words. Write them below. |

_____   _____

_____   _____

Blends
"How Come You Do Me"

Directions: Write the word from the box that starts with the same sound as the picture.

clap	groove	shout	travel	slim	phone

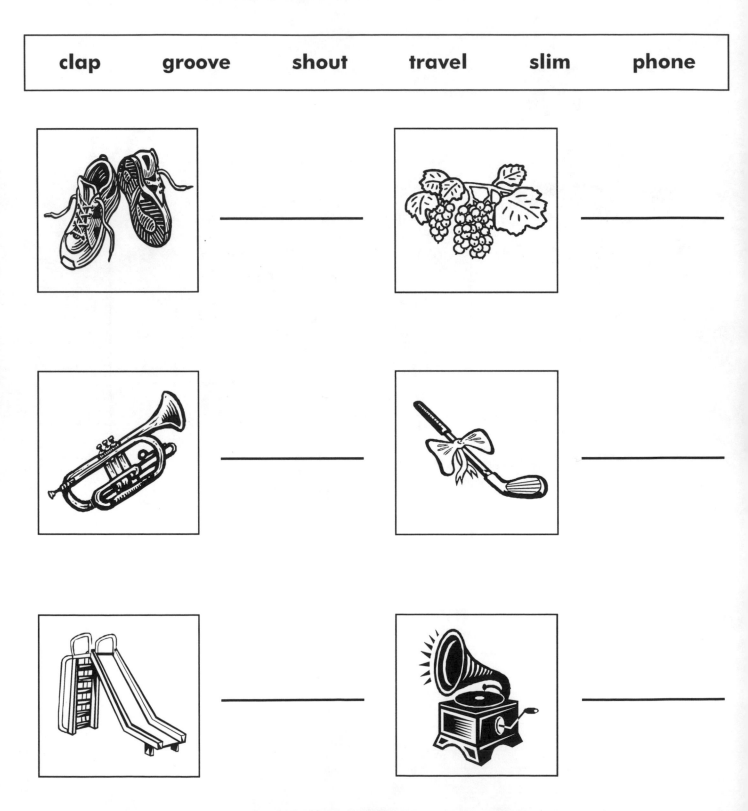

Overview
"School Day Blues"

This story describes the process of writing the Blues. The integrated curriculum is based on <u>first</u> grade curricular concepts.*

<u>Themes</u>:
The themes of this story center on these concepts:
- Rhyming words/word families
- Communities
- Classification
- Graphing
- Facial expressions

<u>Integration of Themes</u>:
The following connections can be made between the curricular concepts and the story line:

- The story teaches students about writing Blues lyrics that relate to the skill of rhyming words and word families. Students can translate this skill to writing poems and song lyrics.

- A discussion of various communities unfolds from the story regarding African American homes. This provides the students with an opportunity to compare and contrast their communities, build models and classify various characteristics of these communities.

- In math, the students will explore the skill of graphing. They can graph their favorite songs, type of homes in their community, number of rhyming families or various other items. The students can also classify graphed data which will further integrate the skills being introduced in science.

- Social skills present the students with an opportunity to explore facial expressions. They can graph how many expressions shown on their faces. They can discuss the meanings and feelings behind facial expressions. Students may want to share facial expressions of various family members or those in their communities.

* The teacher should read the story and then tell it to the class. Next, teach the vocabulary of the story and tell the story again to the class, periodically checking for comprehension.

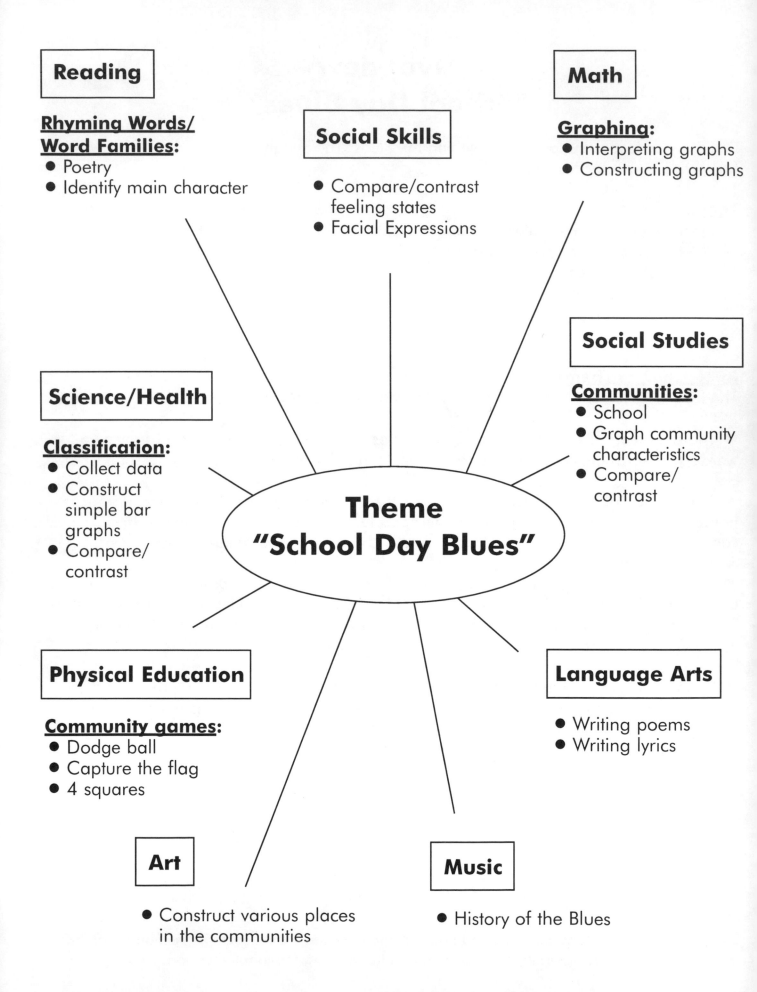

Reading

Rhyming Words/ Word Families:
- Poetry
- Identify main character

Social Skills
- Compare/contrast feeling states
- Facial Expressions

Math

Graphing:
- Interpreting graphs
- Constructing graphs

Science/Health

Classification:
- Collect data
- Construct simple bar graphs
- Compare/ contrast

Social Studies

Communities:
- School
- Graph community characteristics
- Compare/ contrast

Theme "School Day Blues"

Physical Education

Community games:
- Dodge ball
- Capture the flag
- 4 squares

Language Arts
- Writing poems
- Writing lyrics

Art
- Construct various places in the communities

Music
- History of the Blues

22

"School Day Blues"

"School Day Blues" uses a musical form so old that no one knows when it began. The form consists of three sentences - the first two exactly alike, and the third ending with a word that rhymes with the final word in sentences number one and two.

Here are two examples.

1. I'm up with the sun, out the door can't be late.
2. I'm up with the sun, out the door can't be late.
3. I gotta be on time, cause the school bell's gonna ring at eight.

1. I'm sittin on the mailbox, ain't got no time to play.
2. I'm sittin on the mailbox, ain't got no time to play.
3. I hear the sound of brakes, the yellow bus is on its way.

Here is a very old Blues verse from Mississippi that uses the same form:

1. Rock is my pillow and cold ground is my bed.
2. Rock is my pillow and cold ground is my bed.
3. Highway is my home, Lord, I might as well be dead.

The first man to write and publish Blues verses was W.C. Handy. This was during the 1st decade of the 20th century, after he'd heard Blues songs around the Dockery Plantation near Cleveland, Mississippi. Handy was an African-American and felt it was important to jot down the songs of his people. Soon he was making up his own Blues songs.

In 1914, W.C. Handy wrote "St. Louis Blues." One of its verses goes like this:

1. I hate to see that evenin' sun go down.
2. I hate to see that evenin' sun go down.
3. That gal of mine has gone and left this town.

W.C. Handy's "St. Louis Blues" became the most popular Blues of all time and made him a wealthy man. Over 800 different recordings have been made of the song. *Life* magazine reported that England's Queen Elizabeth's favorite dance music was "St. Louis Blues." During World War II, the American Army marched to Glenn Miller's arrangement of "St. Louis Blues." One of the greatest Blues singers of all time, Bessie Smith, considered "St. Louis Blues" her favorite song.

Thirty years before the start of the 20th century, Handy was a small boy in Florence, Alabama. He grew up in what he called "the Negro neighborhood," where music was all around him. "We made rhythm by scraping a twenty penny nail across the teeth of a jawbone of a horse that had died in the woods nearby. We hummed through a fine tooth comb. For drums we wore out our mother's tin pans and pots," he said.

In 1941, in his book, Father of the Blues, W.C. Handy explained that compared to writing other kinds of songs, writing a Blues is easy. He called this three-line lyric form the "classic" Blues form, and felt that anyone could create a Blues verse with a little help. Let's find out if that is true.

Here's another three-line Blues. (Listen to "School Day Blues" again. Sing the Blues below, changing the melody to suit a mood).

1. Hey, Hey, Hey, Hey; Hey, Hey how are you?
2. Hey, Hey, Hey, Hey: Hey, Hey how are you?
3. Do you remember me? I'll bet you do.

Make up a Blues by filling in the last line of each Blues verse below with new words. Don't forget to make the last word in line three rhyme with the last words in lines one and two.

(What's the difference between a true rhyme and a non-rhyme? Circle all the words below that rhyme with "call").

fall---tell---stall---smell---small---bat---bull---mall

Original Blues #1
1. Breezy mornings make me want to play.
2. Breezy mornings make me want to play.
3. (Your words)

Original Blues #2
1. I like to climb, and I like to jump and run.
2. I like to climb, and I like to jump and run.
3. (Your words)

If you completed the above two exercises correctly, you should be proud. Now, like W.C. Handy, B.B. King, Muddy Waters, Willie Dixon, and Ray Charles, you too are a creator of that ancient form of song called the Blues.

Song Lyrics
"School Day Blues"

(2 times)   I'm up with the sun, out the
door can't be late
I gotta be on time cause the
school bell's gonna
ring at 8

(2 times)   I'm sittin' on the mailbox, no
time to play

I hear the sound of brakes,
the yellow bus is on its way

(2 times)   You know my school ain't bad, and I
ain't gonna stop
I think I'll stay right here,
until I make it to the top

When the bell rings at 3 I'll
be heading for the door,
It's been a long day but I'll be back
again for more, walk in my house
feel a little bored, but someone's
knocking at my door and I'll be heading
out once more but I'll home I'm
on the ball, when I hear my mamma call

(2 times)   But when the school day starts
You'll see me walking down the hall
Then being Mayor could be a ball
or maybe I'll just buy city hall

Comprehension
"School Day Blues"

1. Who is the main character of the story?

2. Name one thing he did.

3. Why did W.C. Handy think writing the Blues was easy?

4. Is it true that anyone can create a three-line lyric?

Vocabulary
"School Day Blues"

<u>Directions</u>: Define the following words.

1. rhymes -

2. blues -

3. verse -

4. publish -

5. arrangement -

6. considered -

7. scraping -

8. jawbone -

<u>Directions</u>: Make new words using the blends in the bus window with the work family on the wheels. Write the new words below.

<u>OP</u> words	<u>AY</u> words
_____	_____
_____	_____
_____	_____
_____	_____
_____	_____
_____	_____

Directions: 1. Color the words **YELLOW** that rhyme with **"ALL."**

2. **Write the words on the lines below.**

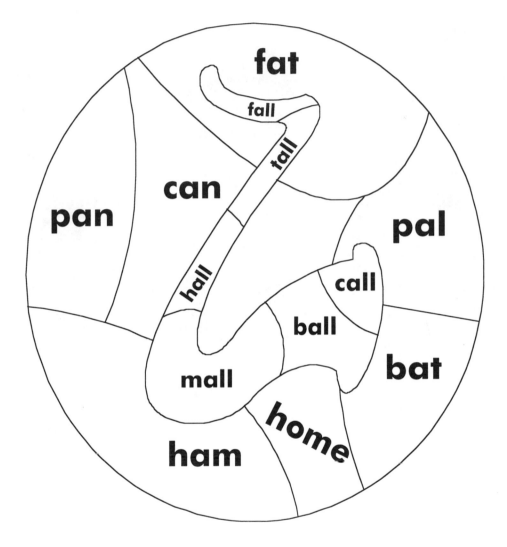

_____   _____

_____   _____

_____   _____

Directions: Find your way home through the snowstorm by following the words that rhyme with **TREE**.

Overview
"When You're Smiling"

This story describes the development process of song writing - call and response and A-B-A form. The integrated curriculum framework is based on <u>second</u> grade curricular concepts.*

Themes:

The themes of this story center around these concepts:

- Writing lyrics/poems
- Community resources
- Observation/classification of data
- Patterns
- Feeling states

Integration of Themes:

The following connections can be made between the curricular concepts and the story line:

- This story centers on feeling states and the emotional response it evokes in others. This lends itself to comparing and contrasting, antonyms/synonyms and understanding of various feeling states. Students begin to understand how their feelings correlate to the feelings of others.

- Throughout all subjects students will be looking for patterns; identifying, classifying and recording. This is apparent in the math concepts as well as through development of an understanding of the scientific method. Students will classify their observations and compare and contrast their likenesses and differences. This concept also applies to their exploration of communities. African villages will be a central focus as the students expand upon the African music found in the story. Rhythmic movements associated with African music will again highlight patterns found in both the music and dance movements.

- Throughout the story the students will encounter proper nouns. This gives them an opportunity to practice identifying and applying this skill to their writing. Students will practice proper nouns in names and communities.

- A culminating activity for this song/unit might be an African ceremony complete with headdresses, a totem pole and music. Students can compare this celebration with the holidays they celebrate as well as their feelings associated with such festivities.

* The teacher should read the story and then tell it to the class. Next, teach the vocabulary of the story and tell the story again to the class, periodically checking for comprehension.

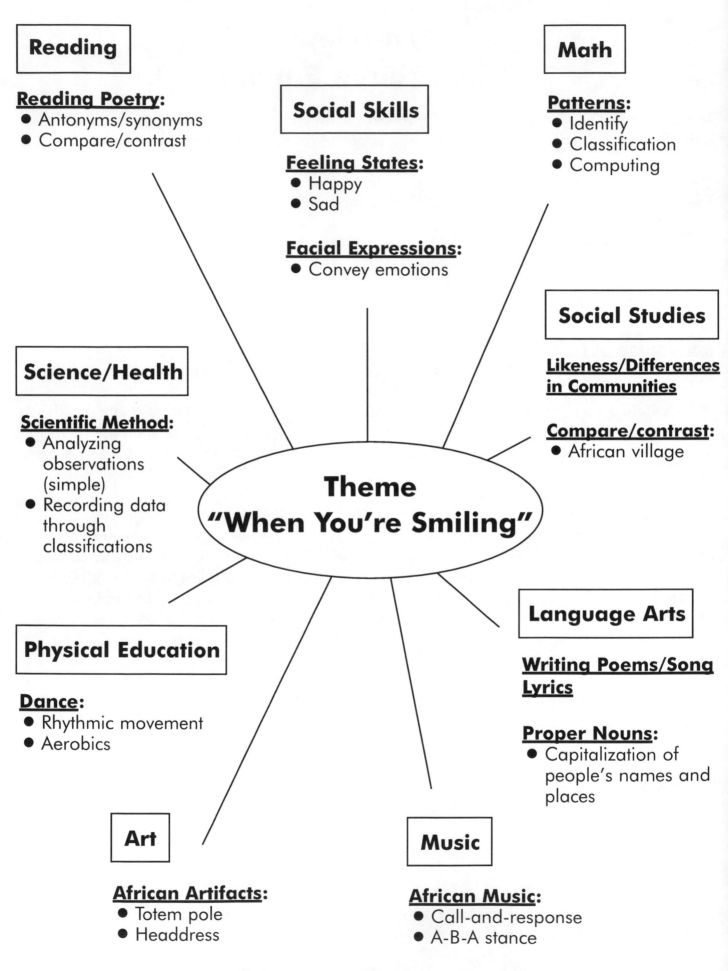

Reading

Reading Poetry:
- Antonyms/synonyms
- Compare/contrast

Social Skills

Feeling States:
- Happy
- Sad

Facial Expressions:
- Convey emotions

Math

Patterns:
- Identify
- Classification
- Computing

Social Studies

Likeness/Differences in Communities

Compare/contrast:
- African village

Science/Health

Scientific Method:
- Analyzing observations (simple)
- Recording data through classifications

Theme "When You're Smiling"

Physical Education

Dance:
- Rhythmic movement
- Aerobics

Language Arts

Writing Poems/Song Lyrics

Proper Nouns:
- Capitalization of people's names and places

Art

African Artifacts:
- Totem pole
- Headdress

Music

African Music:
- Call-and-response
- A-B-A stance

"When You're Smiling"

"When You're Smiling" is a song from the 1920's, designed to lift you up when you're feeling low. In the 1920's, many people felt that the best way to make themselves happy when things weren't going well was to put a smile on their face. If someone looked happy, supposedly they'd begin to feel a little happier.

There were many popular "smile" songs during the 1920's - "Pack Up Your Troubles in your Old Kit Bag and Smile, Smile, Smile," "There Are Smiles That Make You Happy," and "Let a Smile Be Your Umbrella on a Rainy, Rainy Day."

The words of "When You're Smiling" say that 'when you're smiling the whole world smiles with you.' Whether or not that's true, the song is fun to sing. The words appear on the next page. Students might try learning them and singing along with the CD after they've finished reading this story.

Many of the greatest names in jazz and popular music have recorded this song. Louis Armstrong recorded it in 1929 and Louis Prima made it the highlight of his Las Vegas nite-club act in the 1960's. Other great musicians who have recorded the song include King Oliver (one of Louis Armstrong's idols), the band leader, Cab Calloway, and the legendary jazz pianist, Teddy Wilson (who played at the historic 1938 Carnegie Hall Concert with the Benny Goodman Band).

Judy Garland who starred as Dorothy in MGM's "The Wizard of Oz," recorded the song several times and made it an important part of her live concerts. Another famous singer, Frank Sinatra surrounded himself with first rate jazz musicians and also recorded this song.

Why did many great jazz musicians like this song? Maybe it does have the power to make people happy when feeling low. Who knows? You can listen to it and decide for yourself.

*   *   *   *   *   *   *

On the recording, this song uses call-and-response, a device common to African music. In the type of call-and-response used here, the leader sings a phrase and the group echoes him. Try dividing into two groups and chanting the words below in call-and-response style.

	Hey Bop a ree bop
	(Hey bop a ree bop)
(echo)	Hey bop a ree bop
	(Hey bop a ree bop)
	Yes, your baby knows!
	(Yes, your baby knows!)

Students should make up their own call and response lyrics. It's very easy.

*   *   *   *   *   *

"When You're Smiling" is an "A-B-A" song. That means that it begins with a melody (the "A"), switches to a new melody (the "B"), and returns to the original melody (the "A") at the end. The "B" melody is usually called the bridge. In this song, the bridge lyrics are "When you're crying, you bring on the rain. So stop your sighing, be happy again!"

Several of the songs on the CD use variations on the "A-B-A" form. See if you can identify some of them. To make it easier, listen to "It Don't Mean a Thing if it Ain't Got that Swing" while following the printed words. It shouldn't be hard to figure out where the "B" section begins.

*   *   *   *   *   *

When listening to the CD, notice that after "When You're Smiling" is sung once, the alto sax plays the song once, all the way through. His melody is a little different from the melody of the singers on the CD. That is because Al Saunders (the alto saxophonist) "improvises" on the melody. All good jazz musicians improvise. They personalize the melody by adding notes, leaving out notes, or by creating - on the spot - a brand new melody. Some jazz players stay close to the original melody when they improvise, others don't. Listen to the sax solo on this song and decide whether the sax stays close to the melody, moves away from it or does a little of both.

Song Lyrics
"When You're Smiling"

When you're smiling
When you're smiling
The whole world smiles with you

When you're laughing
When you're laughing
The sun comes shining through

But when you're crying
You bring on the rain
Stop you're sighing, be happy again

When you're smiling
When you're smiling
The whole world smiles with you

Comprehension
"When You're Smiling"

1. How does music affect the way we feel? Describe.

2. Why do you think so many musicians recorded the song "When You're Smiling?"

3. What skills are needed to improvise?

4. What are the music patterns in your favorite song?

Vocabulary
"When You're Smiling"

<u>Directions</u>: Define the following words.

1. improvise -

2. echo -

3. idol -

4. legendary -

5. personalize -

6. chant -

7. melody -

8. response -

Patterns
"When You're Smiling"

Directions: Draw what comes next in the pattern.

Example:

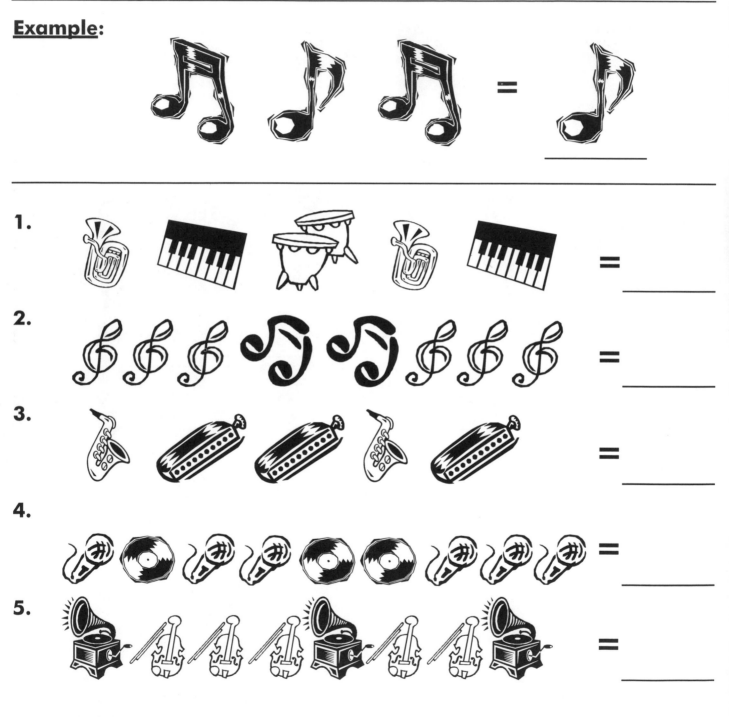

1.

2.

3.

4.

5.

6. **Make your own pattern.**

=

Antonyms and Synonyms
"When You're Smiling"

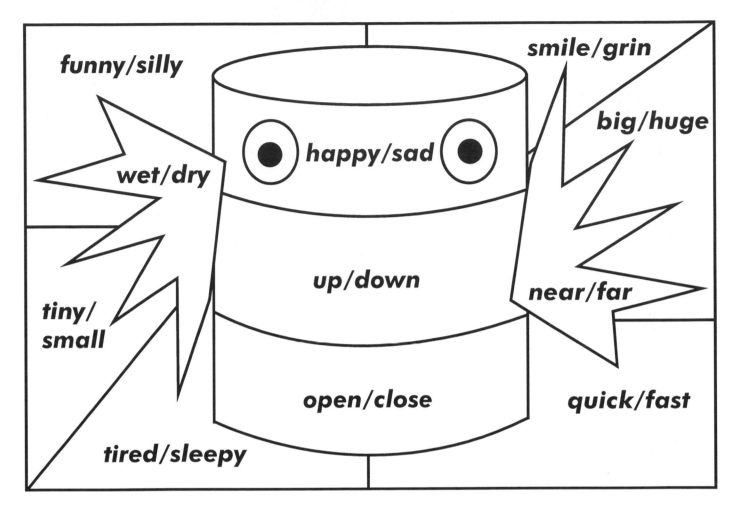

Directions: Color the <u>Antonyms</u> ORANGE. Color the <u>Synonyms</u> BLUE.

Antonyms

_____

_____

_____

_____

_____

Synonyms

_____

_____

_____

_____

_____

_____

Directions: Use the pictures to answer the questions below.

1. Underline the <u>trumpets</u>. How many are there? _____

2. Circle the (saxophone.) How many are there? _____

3. Put an "X" on the DRUMS. How many are there? _____

4. Put a box around the trombones. How many are there? _____

5. Put a star next to the piano keys. How many are there? _____

Step 2: Color the instruments.

Overview
"Zulu Man" (Diga-Diga-Doo)

This story depicts the life story of Dorothy Field's career as a songwriter. The integrated curriculum is based on <u>second</u> grade curricular concepts.*

Themes:
The themes of this story center on these concepts:
- Contribution of women in the workforce
- Comprehending inferences
- Advertisement slogans/adjectives
- Earth's changing surface
- Place value
- Famous women

Integration of Themes:
The following connections can be made between the curricular concepts and the story line:

- Dorothy Fields, through persistence and a positive attitude, was one of the first women songwriters in her time. Her character traits serve as a role model for students and they can emulate Dorothy through their actions. The story describes the value Dorothy placed on education, enabling her to be successful. Through this message students can begin to explore how women entered the workforce and the differences between now and then.

- Throughout the story the author uses very descriptive language, using idioms for the students to interpret. This provides an opportunity to reinforce the skill of understanding inferential information. Students can apply this skill to developing their own idioms and/or advertisement slogans. This is a great time to explore the power of creative language and allow students to integrate the arts into their work.

- Dorothy's career as a songwriter required her to change the culture of both writing lyrics as a man's talent and women's role in society. Science allows us to explore the changes in Earth's surface, which forced us to alter how we adapt. As changes occur we must adapt in order to survive. Integration of this concept with Dorothy's career highlights the ability to change and adapt to various cultural expectations in order to be successful. Further exploration of famous women will enable students to gain a broader understanding of how changes occur in everyday life and are a necessary part of living.

* The teacher should read the story and then tell it to the class. Next, teach the vocabulary of the story and tell the story again to the class, periodically checking for comprehension.

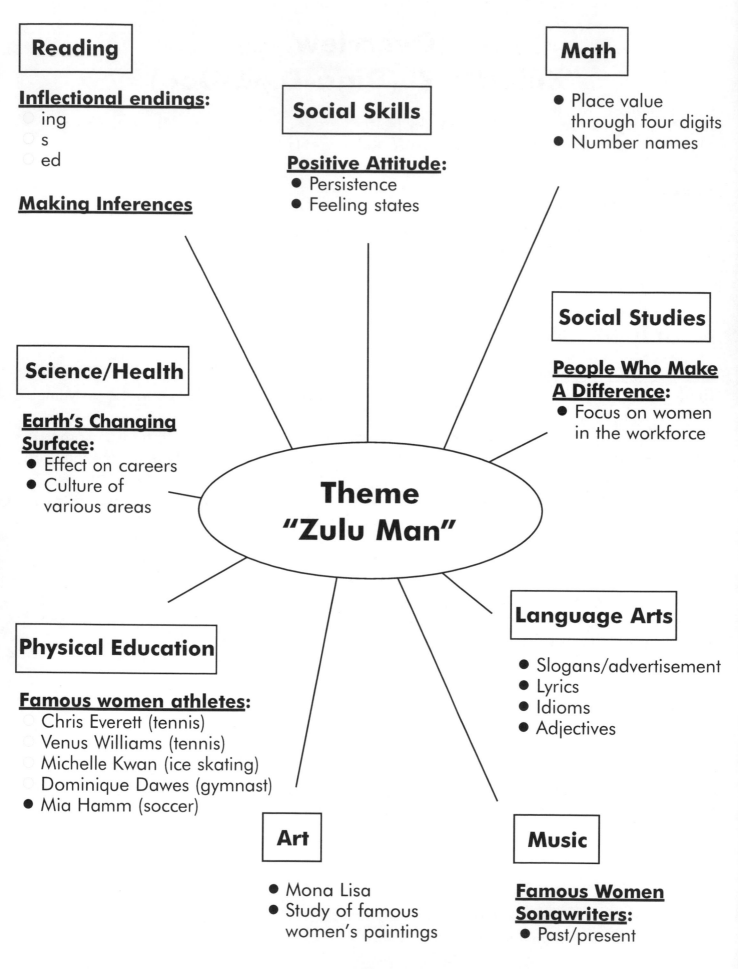

Reading

Inflectional endings:
○ ing
○ s
○ ed

Making Inferences

Social Skills

Positive Attitude:
● Persistence
● Feeling states

Math

● Place value through four digits
● Number names

Social Studies

People Who Make A Difference:
● Focus on women in the workforce

Science/Health

Earth's Changing Surface:
● Effect on careers
● Culture of various areas

Theme "Zulu Man"

Language Arts

● Slogans/advertisement
● Lyrics
● Idioms
● Adjectives

Physical Education

Famous women athletes:
○ Chris Everett (tennis)
○ Venus Williams (tennis)
○ Michelle Kwan (ice skating)
○ Dominique Dawes (gymnast)
● Mia Hamm (soccer)

Art

● Mona Lisa
● Study of famous women's paintings

Music

Famous Women Songwriters:
● Past/present

"Zulu Man"* (Diga-Diga-Doo)

"Diga-Diga-Doo" was the song that began Dorothy Fields' career as a songwriter. In the first half of the 20th century, she was America's only <u>major</u> woman song lyricist.

In a 1962 interview, after she'd temporarily retir<u>ed</u>, Fields was asked why there hadn't been more women songwriters in her day. When asked if men had more talent than women, Fields insisted, "I do <u>not</u> think men have more talent than women!" She went on to explain that, when she was young, women were encouraged to marry, clean the house, wash the husband's' clothes, and take care of the children. In addition, women needed to cook for the family, shop for groceri<u>es</u>, entertain visitors, and make every member of the family feel welcome, worthwhile, and wise. Not much time was left for song writing. In Fields' time, the song writing business was essentially a me<u>n</u>'s club. No women were allowed - at least not as <u>full-time</u> members.

But Fields <u>broke down the doors</u> of that men's club and wrote the lyrics of great songs still popular with jazz artist<u>s</u> 70 years after they were written. She could find just the right words to describe the excitement felt when getting ready for a date with someone you really love.

> "Someday, when I'm awfully low,
> When the world is cold,
> I will feel a glow
> Just thinking of you
> And the way you look tonight."

Fields won the Academy Award for "Best Song in a Film" for these lyrics in 1936. The film entitled "Swing Time," starred Fred Astaire and Ginger Rogers. Since then, "The Way You Look Tonight" has been recorded by more than 100 artists, including Fred Astaire, Billie Holliday, Benny Goodman, Ella Fitzgerald, and Louis Armstrong.

When asked in an interview whether Fields' song writing required her to study, she replied, "Of course. I've always had a healthy respect for the <u>power of words</u>. I never stop studying. I don't believe that anyone's education <u>ever</u> stops."

Song writing didn't always come easily to Fields, but she felt that almost anything was possible with hard work and persistence. Failure never stopped her from trying. In her song, "Pick Yourself Up," she wrote:

> "Nothing's impossible
> I have found,
> For when your chin
> Is on the ground,

You pick yourself up
And dust yourself off . . .
And start all over again."

Fields had a sense of humor. In a song about a boy who was too slow to show his girl affection, she wrote:

"A fine romance,
My friend, this is,
A fine romance
With no kisses!"

In 1930, Fields wrote the lyrics for a Louis Armstrong song hit called, "On the <u>Sunny Side of the Street</u>." The lyrics begin with:

"Grab your coat and get your hat,
Leave your worries on the doorstep.
Life can be so sweet,
On the sunny side of the street."

That trip to the sunny side of the street forced Fields to <u>dodge a lot of traffic on the way</u>, but she made it.

The lyrics of one of Fields' longest-lived hit songs grew out of something that happened to her one day in New York City in 1927. Fields saw a young woman and her boyfriend holding hands, gazing into Tiffany's Jewelry Store window on Fifth Avenue. The woman's clothes were patched and worn. She looked very poor, but she turned to her boyfriend and said, "I wish you could buy me one of those diamond bracelets."

Fields felt sorry for the woman until the boyfriend spoke. His words made Fields run to get a notebook and turn the young man's comments into part of a song lyric. He'd said, "I'm sorry, . . . I can't give you anything but love, Baby!" Fields eliminated "I'm sorry" and added, "It's the only thing I've plenty of, Baby!" The song, "I Can't Give You Anything But Love" reached number one on the Billboard charts in October, 1928 and was one of the top ten hits of the entire year. A favorite song of jazz great Louis Armstrong, he recorded it several times and sang it in his 1945 film "Jam Session."

* The title of the song Dorothy Fields wrote, and some of the lyrics of "Diga-Diga-Doo" were changed on the CD to make them easier for children to sing.

Song Lyrics
"Zulu Man"

Zulu Man is feeling blue, feel his
heart beat like a drum
diga-diga-doo   diga-diga-doo
diga-diga-doo   diga-doo

Zulu Man got out his horn and played
the blues for all to hear
diga-diga-doo   diga-diga-doo
diga-diga-doo   diga-doo

Zulu Man is feeling blue
Feel is heart beat like a drum
diga-diga-doo   diga-diga-doo
diga-diga-doo   diga-doo

Feel that earth move with his rhythm
Brings out everything that's in him

Zulu Man is feeling blue, feel his
heart beat like a drum
diga-diga-doo   diga-diga-doo
diga-diga-doo   diga-doo

Comprehension
"Zulu Man"

1. How have women's roles changed since the first half of the 20th century?

2. What does Dorothy say about education?

3. How did hard work help Dorothy become successful?

4. How has Dorothy's success as a songwriter been a role model for female songwriters today? (i.e. B. Spears)

Vocabulary
"Zulu Man"

Directions: Define the following words.

1. career -

2. songwriter -

3. lyricist -

4. interviewer -

5. encouraged -

6. gazing -

7. lyric -

8. eliminated -

Adding "ing"
"Zulu Man"

Rule: If a word ends in "e," drop the "e" and add "ing."

Directions: Write the word that finishes the sentence.

write   smile   gaze

hope   come   love

1. Is Zulu man _____ with us to school?

2. When you're _____ you're not blue.

3. Dorothy saw a girl _____ out the window.

4. I am _____ for a trumpet for my birthday.

5. Tom is _____ his new puppy.

6. We are _____ a new song.

Directions: Color the picture. Then, write a story describing Dorothy.

Dorothy is a _____ woman. The

color of her hat is _____. She likes

to sing _____ songs. She likes to

wear _____ dresses. I like Dorothy

because she is so _____.

<u>Directions</u>: Draw a picture to describe the phrases below.

<u>Example</u>: Leave your worries on the doorstep.

1. <u>The sunny side of the street.</u>

2. <u>I'm awfully low.</u>

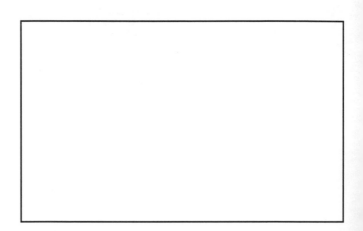

3. <u>When your chin is on the ground, pick yourself up.</u>

4. <u>The power of words.</u>

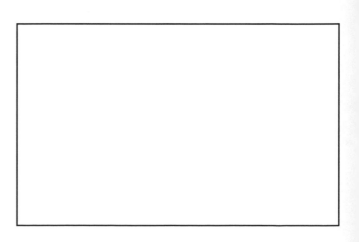

Overview
"Listen to the Jazz Band"

This story describes the origin of the New Orleans jazz style and word origins associated with jazz. The integrated curriculum is based on <u>third</u> grade curricular concepts.*

Themes:

The themes of this story center on these concepts:

- Word origins - prefixes/suffixes
- Industrial revolution
- Life cycle
- Estimation
- Cooperative competition

Integration of Themes:

The following connections can be made between the curricular concepts and the story line:

- The story discusses how musicians obtained flawed instruments from manufacturers. This provides an opportunity to discuss the changes brought forth by the industrial revolution and the effects it had on society. Comparison between life before and after the revolution will enable students to see the great impact this time period had on developing technology. Estimation of product development timelines, cost of production and availability of goods and services provides an integration of math skills.

- Another theme in the story pertains to the style of jazz music in New Orleans. Comparison of funeral processions affords students an opportunity to view different cultural practices. Word origin is discussed to further elaborate on the jazz culture. Students can connect this with word origins as they relate to suffixes and prefixes found throughout the story. The song provides the students with a mini lesson in French as part of the lyrics are repeated in French. Multi-culturalism is apparent throughout this story and song.

- Competition is related in the story to the musician's performance during the funeral procession. Typically we do not think of competition in this manner. This expands our students understanding of this term. Teaching students cooperative competition is a social skill they will need to acquire and use throughout life. It is oftentimes a difficult skill to master. Presentation of this skill through various content matter reinforces its significance.

* The teacher should read the story and then tell it to the class. Next, teach the vocabulary of the story and tell the story again to the class, periodically checking for comprehension.

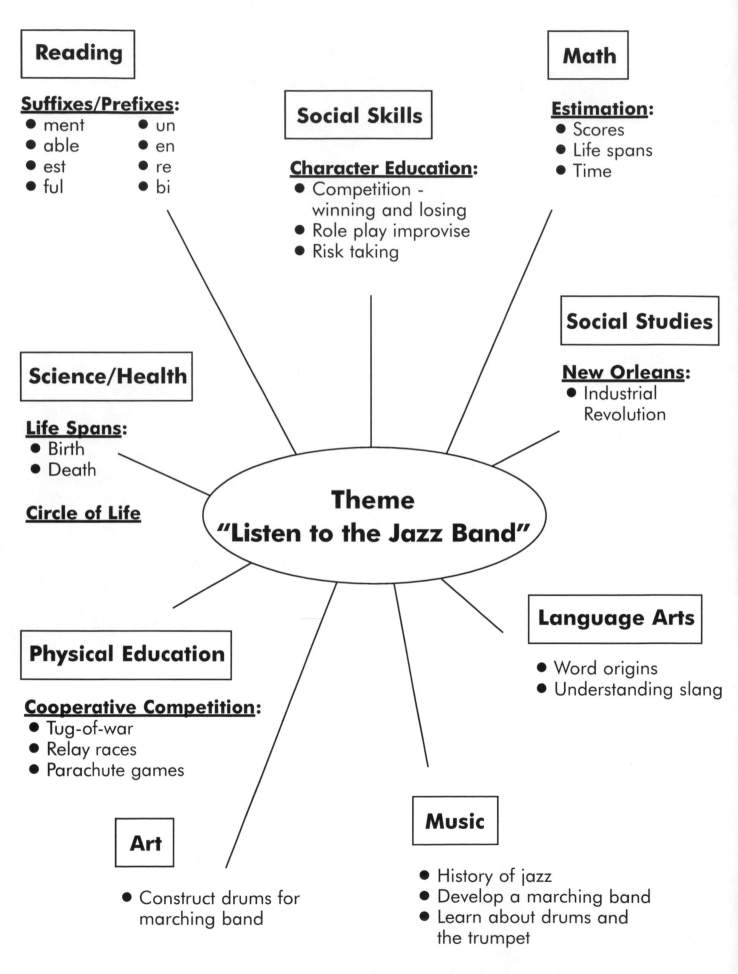

Reading

Suffixes/Prefixes:
- ment
- able
- est
- ful
- un
- en
- re
- bi

Social Skills

Character Education:
- Competition - winning and losing
- Role play improvise
- Risk taking

Math

Estimation:
- Scores
- Life spans
- Time

Science/Health

Life Spans:
- Birth
- Death

Circle of Life

Social Studies

New Orleans:
- Industrial Revolution

Theme "Listen to the Jazz Band"

Language Arts

- Word origins
- Understanding slang

Physical Education

Cooperative Competition:
- Tug-of-war
- Relay races
- Parachute games

Art

- Construct drums for marching band

Music

- History of jazz
- Develop a marching band
- Learn about drums and the trumpet

"Listen to the Jazz Band"

Listen to the Jazz Band uses 19th century marching band melodies played in the early jazz style - the style of jazz's home, New Orleans. Why, out of all the cities in America did New Orleans become the birthplace of jazz?

New Orleans, originally a French city, placed high value on music. America's first resident opera company appeared in New Orleans before 1800. The French created many marching bands. Long before the Civil War, African-Americans joined these marching bands, forming marching bands of their own. Drum playing by African-Americans was forbidden on the East Coast plantations because the masters feared the power of the drum. But the French in New Orleans set up Place Congo where African-Americans were encouraged to bring their own drums on Sundays (their day off) to play, sing, and dance together.

There's another reason New Orleans was a musical town: French instrument manufacturers like Selmer, Erhard, and Boucher discovered they could have their instruments made less expensively in New Orleans. They set up small factories, staffed mostly by African-Americans. (This is a little like what U.S. companies do today in third-world countries). When the instruments were slightly flawed, instead of shipping them to Paris, they gave them away. Musical instruments were so easily obtainable in New Orleans that many of its residents owned one and could play one.

The New Orleans jazz style probably originated during a funeral service. That may sound strange, but here's what New York Times jazz critic, Charles Edward Smith, said: "In New Orleans funerals, the brass band is preceded by an honor guard with flags. The band does not enter the cemetery. At the gates the band separates into two sections, facing each other on either side of the entrance, playing the slow marches that, as Louis Armstrong remarked, 'could just touch your heart, they were so beautiful.' After the funeral, there was a roll on the snare drum, a blast of the trumpet, and the lively jazz cheered up the mourners and set them to dancing back to town with the marching band."

These jazz concerts were improvised - that is, the music was changed to suit the moods of the players, created on the spot. No one, including the musicians, knew what would happen next, which added to the excitement and fun.

A famous classical composer named Aaron Copland was fascinated by jazz and he wrote, "When you improvise, you take risks and can't foretell the results. In jazz, five or six musicians improvise simultaneously. This is its charm."

Another way for a band to take a risk was the "cutting" contest. In the early 1900s, a jazz band would often play on the back of a horse-drawn wagon, driving through town creating a movable concert. As the band played, people would run behind the bandwagon.

Sometimes, a band driving in one direction passed a band driving in another direction. The leaders of each band would challenge the other.

The tailgates of the two wagons were tied together so no one could escape after the contest had begun. Each band had to alternate playing the same tune. The crowd would decide which band was better and the winners were loudly applauded.

The trombonist stayed at the end of the wagon, beside the tailgate. This prevented his slide from poking out the eyes of his fellow band members. In New Orleans, they still call the trombone the tailgate trombone.

Cutting, by the way, didn't always involve two whole bands, so sometimes two trumpet players would alternate improvisations to see who was better. Old-time New Orleans jazz player, Edmund Hall, said that he once saw a trumpet player cut so badly that he threw his horn to the ground and walked off defeated and disgusted.

Usually cutting didn't upset anyone. It was a musical sport, and when the contest was over, the two small bands would often jump up to make a larger band, playing one song together before they parted.

Ever wonder where the word "jazz" comes from? Many different explanations have been given; but this one probably goes back to the very first use of the word. In 19th century French-speaking New Orleans, when a dancer or a musician performed with great skill, he was called "Chezz-beau" (shezz bow). Chezz meant chair or throne, and beau meant boy or young man. The young man on the throne, of course, is a king, and chezz beau, which eventually became jazz-bo, was a term to describe the king of musicians, singers or dancers. Sometime early in the 20th century, we started calling jazz-bo's music "jazz." We still call it that today.

Song Lyrics
"Listen to the Jazz Band"

(2 times)   Just listen to the trombone, Just listen
to the jazz
No other kind of music makes me feel
that way
ECOUTE VRAIMENT LA TROMPETTE, ECOUTE
VRAIMENT LE JAZZ,
AUCUNE AUTRE MUSIQUE ME FAIT CET EFFET

(2 times)   Just listen to the clarinet, just listen
to the jazz
No other kind of music makes me
feel that way

Comprehension
"Listen to the Jazz Band"

1. Explain why flawed instruments were easily obtainable by residents of New Orleans.

2. Describe the differences between a funeral in New Orleans and a traditional funeral.

3. Why is "cutting" a musical sport and what role did improvisation play?

4. Explain the origin of the word jazz.

Vocabulary
"Listen to the Jazz Band"

Directions: Define the following words.

1. melodies -

2. plantations -

3. manufacturers -

4. flawed -

5. obtainable -

6. improvised -

7. mourners -

8. simultaneously -

Prefixes and Suffixes
"Listen to the Jazz Band"

Directions: Complete the crossword puzzle using the words below.

excitement   unusual

movable   encourage

slowest   reappear

beautiful   bicycle

ACROSS:

1. able to be moved
2. act of being excited
3. not usual
4. to make courage

DOWN:

1. appear again
2. full of beauty
3. two cycles
4. the most slow

Estimation
"Listen to the Jazz Band"

Directions: Compute each word problem by finding the **AVERAGE**.

Example: Aaron scored two runs in the first baseball game, four runs in his second game and six runs in his third game. How many runs did he average?

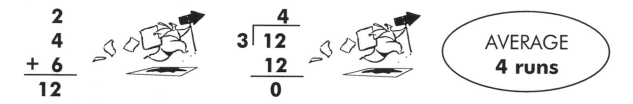

$$
\begin{array}{r} 2 \\ 4 \\ + 6 \\ \hline 12 \end{array}
\qquad
3\,\overline{\smash{)}\,\begin{array}{r} 4 \\ 12 \\ 12 \\ \hline 0 \end{array}}
$$

AVERAGE
4 runs

1. Louis went bowling. He obtained scores of 110, 132 and 70. What is his average score?

2. Selmer, Erhard and Boucher ran a relay race. Their scores were 15 seconds, 21 seconds and 12 seconds. What was their average score?

3. Teams one, two and three were playing beachball parachute. Team one kept the ball on the parachute for six seconds, team two for nine seconds and team three for 12 seconds. What was their average time?

4. Charles scored 20, 16, 32 and 24 points in four basketball games. How many points did he average?

French
"Listen to the Jazz Band"

Directions: Practice the lines from the song in French.

1. <u>Just listen to the jazz band</u>
   Ecoutez donc le groupe de jazz

2. <u>Just listen to the jazz</u>
   Ecoutez donc le jazz

3. <u>No other kind of music makes me feel that way</u>
   Aucune autre musique ne me fait cet effet

4. <u>Just listen to the trumpet</u>
   Ecoutez donc la trompette

5. <u>Just listen to the clarinet</u>
   Ecoutez donc la clarinette

Step 2: Practice these new French words and phrases.

1. <u>hello</u>
   Salut

2. <u>goodbye</u>
   Au revoir

3. <u>school</u>
   Ecole

4. <u>car</u>
   Auto

5. <u>What is your name?</u>
   **Quel est votre nom
   (ton)**

6. <u>My name is</u> _____.
   Mon nom est _____.
   (or) **Je m'apelle** _____.

7. <u>How are you</u>?
   **Comment allez-vous
   vas-tu**

8. <u>How old are you</u>?
   **Quel age avez-vous
   as-tu**

60

Overview
"Sing, Sing, Sing"

This story describes the first jazz concert ever played at Carnegie Hall and the cultural change that resulted. The integrated curriculum is based on <u>third</u> grade curricular concepts.*

Themes:
The themes of this story center on these concepts:
- Understanding environmental expectation
- Identifying cultural differences
- Units of measurement
- Place value
- Comprehending inferences

Integration of Themes:
The following connections can be made between the curricular concepts and the story line:

- The story describes how the jazz concept at Carnegie Hall altered America's attitude towards jazz forever. The behavior typically associated with Carnegie Hall was changed. This provides an opportunity for students to explore behavioral expectations of various cultures and environments. Cultural diversity can be discussed in review of this event and the role it plays in society today. Students can role play various ways of altering their behaviors in response to the environmental expectations (playground, school, library, and mall).

- The concert was filled to capacity, with some people standing in the back. The concepts of volume, mass, time and distance can be integrated with the story line. Students can practice writing numerals and reinforcing their concept of place value. Physical education can further integrate these concepts through measurement of track and field events.

- The ability to make inferences is a skill that can be integrated into Language Arts through trying to interpret what the author was saying about the concert. Use of descriptors (adjectives and adverbs) not only adds interest to the story but enables the reader to visualize the concert in greater detail. This story is a good example of not only inferential meaning but includes many descriptions the students can incorporate into their writing, drawings or other art forms.

* The teacher should read the story and then tell it to the class. Next, teach the vocabulary of the story and tell the story again to the class, periodically checking for comprehension.

Reading
- Understanding inferences
- Making predictions

Social Skills
- Understanding environmental expectations
- Adapting to the environment

Math
- Place value to 4 digits
- Writing numerals in expanded formation

Science/Health
- Measuring units of volume, mass, time and distance

Social Studies
- Recognize culture of different groups
- Identify how cultures change

Theme "Sing, Sing, Sing"

Physical Education

Track and Field:
- Sprints
- Long jumps
- Timings

Language Arts
- Adjectives/adverbs

Art
- Develop imagery evoked pieces through listening to various instrumental pieces

Music
- Develop the connection between emotions and musical selections

"Sing, Sing, Sing"

"Sing, Sing, Sing" was the high point in one of the most important concerts in the history of Jazz. The concert took place on the evening of January 16, 1938, on the stage of New York's Carnegie Hall.

Many people were shocked to hear that a jazz concert was being played at Carnegie Hall. How dare they? The music of great European composers like Beethoven, Mozart and Bach had been played there, by the greatest classical musicians in the world. A jazz concert would disgrace that sacred stage. Nonetheless, a jazz concert was planned.

When January 16th arrived, the thousands of seats in that huge auditorium were filled. People stood outside begging to get in. Tickets were sold for the standing room in the back of the theater and, when that was filled, people sat on the floor below the stage. Even before the music began, excitement flowed through the hall like electricity.

The audience was dressed in the usual attire for Carnegie Hall in those days - tuxedos and evening gowns. Though they didn't want to wrinkle their evening attire, they squeezed close to each other on the cold floor, anyway, just grateful to witness jazz history.

This was not only the first important jazz concert in Carnegie Hall, it was apparently the first important integrated jazz concert in the hall. Jazz Magazine, Downbeat, reported, "The musicians were nervous. When it actually became 8:45, time to go on stage, nobody wanted to go out first." The New York Sun wrote, "Whether the local seismograph recorded it or not, an earthquake of violent intensity rocked a small corner of Manhattan last night as swing took Carnegie Hall."

The concert was played by the Benny Goodman Band supplemented by members of the Duke Ellington Band, including the sensational jazz saxophonist, Johnny Hodges. At one point in the concert, jazz pianist Count Basie, made a guest appearance, along with the cool tenor saxophonist player, Lester Young. All the Ellington and Basie personnel were African-American, as were the arrangers and several members of Goodman's own band. The music alternated between Big Band jazz and small group jazz, constantly keeping the audience in a state of suspense. "What's next?" someone might have asked. The answer could only be, "Who knows?"

"Sing, Sing, Sing" was the wildest and largest piece played at the Carnegie Hall concert. It's climax was a ferocious solo by Goodman's drummer, Gene Krupa. People became so excited that they couldn't remain seated. Movie films recorded formally dressed men and women stomping their feet, snapping their fingers and shouting, "Go, Benny, go!" and "Gene, you send me!" This was not the kind of subdued behavior expected at Carnegie Hall. It helped change America's attitude toward jazz forever. Though jazz was less restrained than classical music, it was, nonetheless, an important American art form. The other creators of today's serious jazz owe a debt to Benny Goodman's historic jazz concert that evening.

Once The *Jazzing Up Instruction* version of "Sing, Sing, Sing" is heard, listen to the original version by the Benny Goodman Band. It has remained in print ever since it was first recorded in 1938. If interested, this version can be ordered from any record store:

Live at Carnegie Hall 1938
Columbia Records
CD #65143

Song Lyrics
"Sing, Sing, Sing"

Sing, Sing, Sing everybody start to sing
Sing it loud, sing it soft, now you're
singing with a swing

Sing, Sing, Sing everybody start to sing
Heidi Hi Hoodi Ho now you're singing
with a swing

When the band comes down the street
Everybody's on their feet
and when a jazz band starts a groove
everybody's "In the Mood."

Sing, Sing, Sing everybody start to sing
sing it loud, sing it soft, now you're
singing with a swing

Comprehension
"Sing, Sing, Sing"

1. Why do you think people were so interested in attending the Jazz concert at Carnegie Hall?

2. Describe how the attire of the audience did not match the environment (Carnegie Hall).

3. Explain the cultural change that resulted from the Jazz concert on January 16, 1938.

4. What did the author mean by "An earthquake of violent intensity rocked a small corner of Manhattan last night?"

Vocabulary
"Sing, Sing, Sing"

<u>Directions</u>: Define the following words.

1. attire -

2. seismograph -

3. supplement -

4. personnel -

5. climax -

6. subdued -

7. ferocious -

8. disgrace -

Adjectives and Adverbs
"Sing, Sing, Sing"

Rules: Adjectives are words that describe the noun. Adverbs are words that describe the verb.

Directions: Underline the adjective and circle the adverb in each of the following sentences.

Example: The <u>pretty</u> girl danced (quickly.)

     Adjective   Adverb

1. The handsome man stomped his feet noisily.

2. She lost her sparkly purse somewhere.

3. Benny's ferocious performance shook the auditorium violently.

4. The formally dressed audience shouted loudly after the performance.

Step 2: Create <u>two</u> sentences on your own. Include an adjective and adverb in <u>each</u> sentence.

1. _____

2. _____

Place Value: Thousands
"Sing, Sing, Sing"

Directions: Use the codes below to color the hall.

If the number has . . .

4 thousands - color it <u>RED</u>

8 thousands - color it <u>GREEN</u>

7 thousands - color it <u>ORANGE</u>

3 hundreds - color it <u>YELLOW</u>

9 tens - color it <u>BLUE</u>

2 tens - color it <u>BROWN</u>

1 one - color it <u>PINK</u>

5 ones - color it <u>PURPLE</u>

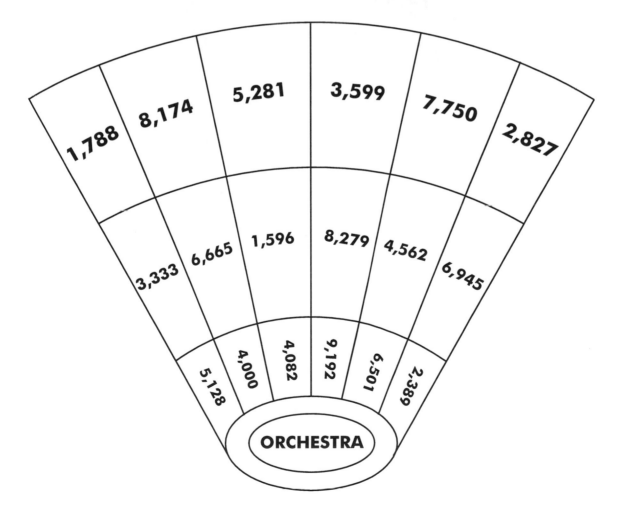

Directions: Read the story. Follow the instructions and answer the questions below.

The jazz musicians are performing at Carnegie Hall tonight. The show begins at 8:45 p.m. The musicians will rehearse for the performance at 4:30 p.m. Rehearsal is over at 5:30 p.m. They will eat dinner at 6:30 p.m. The musicians have to be at Carnegie Hall at 8:15 p.m. to get dressed and ready for the performance. However, they would like to relax before the show.

1. Use a BLUE crayon to draw performance time on the clock.

2. Use an ORANGE crayon to draw when rehearsal begins.

3. How long is rehearsal?

4. Use a RED crayon to draw dinner time on the clock.

5. What do the performers want to do after dinner?

6. How much time do you think the performers will have to relax?

Overview
"Everybody Loves My Baby"

This story describes life during the 1920's and how it came to be known as "The Roaring Twenties." The integrated curriculum is based on <u>fourth</u> grade curricular concepts.*

Themes:
The themes of this story center on these concepts:
- The Roaring Twenties
- Math reasoning skills
- Reading with expression
- Etiquette
- Drug awareness

Integration of Themes:
The following connections can be made between the curricular concepts and the story line:

- The story describes The Roaring Twenties and the changes that occurred in women's roles both in the family and society. Students can compare and contrast how women were perceived before the 1920's with today. During this time period teenagers made up their own language, similar to present teenagers. Students will enjoy hearing the past slang and comparing it to the slang used today. Speak-easies became popular and women were frequenting bars. This affords an opportunity to teach about drug awareness/prevention.

- As the role of women changed proper etiquette changed as well. Respect for authority was apparent in the story, however change was occurring. Reinforcement of good manners and respect for authority naturally flows from this story. This is a good opportunity for role playing. Students can practice reading with expression and integrating that skill to written expression using various forms of punctuation. Understanding facial expressions is often like trying to understand a code. Students can explore this concept in math while they try to integrate their problem solving strategies by unraveling word problems.

- The Roaring Twenties was a time of change. It was a lively time! Fashion changed, dances changed and so did music. Students will enjoy comparing and contrasting fashions and practicing popular dances.

* For students who do not possess the reading skills necessary to read the story the teacher, or one of the students should read the story and tell it to them. Next, teach the vocabulary of the story and read the story aloud to the students who lack the reading skills necessary to read it themselves.

Reading

Reading with Expression:
- Plays
- Roles
- Characterization

Social Skills

- Etiquette
- Manners
- Respect for authority

Math

Reasoning/Word Problems:
- Codes
- Puzzles

Social Studies

Roaring Twenties:
- Compare/contrast
- Women's role

Science/Health

Drug Awareness:
- Alcohol
- Smoking
- Drugs

Theme "Everybody Loves My Baby"

Language Arts

Punctuation:
- Question mark
- Exclamation
- Quotation marks
- Commas
- Periods

Physical Education

Aerobics:
- Pulse monitoring
- Cardiovascular workouts

Art

History of Fashion:
- 1920's
- Design an outfit
- Make an outfit

Music

Charleston:
- Music
- Dance

"Everybody Loves My Baby"

The song, "Everybody Loves My Baby," appeared in 1924 and instantly became popular. The song was written by an African-American pianist from New Orleans named Spencer Williams. Louis Armstrong recorded this song that year on the Okeh Label. "Everybody Loves My Baby" was one of Louis Armstrong's earliest hits, becoming one of the most popular songs of the 1920's.

The 1920's was a time when young people were developing a language of their own, their own way of behaving. Some people called this time in history <u>The Roaring Twenties</u> because, for many, life seemed to be a day-in, day-out party. With music now on the newly invented radio, people were dancing on the living room rug, while women were behaving in a shocking manner. Women frequented speak-easies, drank at bars beside men, bobbed their hair, wore short dresses, and occasionally smoked cigarettes in public. None of these behaviors were commonplace among women <u>before</u> the 1920's. Here's a picture of teenage life in the 1920's - the story of 15 year old Millie.

<u>"Everybody Loves My Millie"</u>

Charlie sat in the swing on Millie's front porch, strumming his ukulele and singing -

> "Everybody loves my Millie
> But my Millie don't love nobody but me
> Nobody but me!"

Millie slammed the screen door on her way out. "Charlie," she said, "you're such an egotist! What makes you think I love nobody but you?"

"It's just a song," said Charlie.

"Good," said Millie, "because I'm having too much fun to go steady with you or anyone else."

He sang the song again, with the right words -

> "Everybody loves my baby
> But my baby don't love nobody but me
> Nobody but me."

"Charlie," said Millie, "shouldn't it be 'my baby <u>doesn't</u> love <u>anybody</u> but me'?"

"Don't blame me, Millie" Charlie said. "I didn't write the song. It's the times we live in. In 1924, good grammar is for old maid school teachers. Breaking the rules is copacetic."

"Yeah," said Millie sarcastically. "It's the cat's meow."

"Guess what I got today?" asked Charlie.

"A flagpole for you to sit on and break shipwreck Kelly's record."

"No," said Charlie. "What _is_ his record?"

"Forty-nine days, on the boardwalk in Atlantic City," Millie answered.

"I have no ambish to do that," Charlie said.

"You're too intel to do that," Millie said.

"You too, Mil," said Charlie.

"Esyay, I essgay you're ightray," Millie said.

"Don't speak pig Latin, Mil. You know I can't understand it," Charlie said.

Millie paused as she pulled back her blonde waves and hid them behind her head. "Charlie, should I bob my hair?"

"Oh my God, what would your mother say?" Charlie said.

"She's already bobbed hers. It's my father I'm worried about," said Millie.

"It's a big decision. Once you're scalped, that's it. You have to live with it," Charlie added.

"Well, you can't be a flapper without bobbed hair," Millie teased.

"Why can't you?" Charlie questioned.

"Because," Millie sputtered, obviously flustered at having to make sense out of her opinion. "Oh, Charlie," she said, fidgeting on the porch, "play the Charleston on your uke."

"I don't know it," Charlie said.

"Fake it," Millie said.

Charlie began to play "Everybody Loves My Baby" (the only song he knew how to play) in the closest thing to a Charleston rhythm he could muster.

"How's that?" he asked.

Millie didn't need to answer. She was bending her knees and shuffling her feet in something that was as closely related to the Charleston as was Charlie's uke playing. The two of them sped up the rhythm and began laughing as she danced and he played.

Suddenly, the screen door opened, and there, very tall and straight in his old-fashioned walrus moustache and open celluloid collar was Millie's father, not looking entirely pleased.

Charlie and Millie instantly stopped what they were doing, froze and faked their best innocent smiles.

Millie's father shook his head, and said "Young people! They're runnin' wild."

Charlie gulped and said, "Speaking of running, it's time for me to get home. Good night, sir. Good night, Millie." He rose and paddled his way home with his ukulele.

"What ever happened to propriety?" said Millie's father. "When your mother was your age, I couldn't sit on the porch with her without a chaperone."

"Father," said Millie, "when are you going to catch up with 1924?"

"Some things," Millie's father said, "are fads. They're part and parcel of 1924. But some things are the same, whether it's 1824 or 1924. Right is right."

"Right," said Millie.

"Good night," said Millie's father.

"Good night, father."

The screen door slammed behind him and Millie sat on the porch swing, thinking about whether she should bob her hair. "Maybe," she thought. "Then again, maybe not. I'll decide tomorrow."

Song Lyrics
"Everybody Loves My Baby"

Everybody loves my baby
but my baby don't love nobody
but me, nobody but me

Everybody loves my baby
but my baby don't want
nobody but me - nobody but me

Everybody loves my baby
but my baby don't love nobody
but me - nobody but me

Comprehension
"Everybody Loves My Baby"

1. What is meant by <u>The Roaring Twenties</u>?

2. How did the changes in the 1920's contribute to the fads that emerged?

3. What are the current fads and what effect will the 21st century have on them?

4. Compare/contrast slang from the 1920's to today.

Vocabulary
"Everybody Loves My Baby"

Directions: Define the following words.

1. Speak-easies -

2. flustered -

3. fidgeting -

4. fads -

5. propriety -

6. chaperone -

7. parcel -

8. egotist -

Directions: Solve the problems below. Write the correct answer in the box.

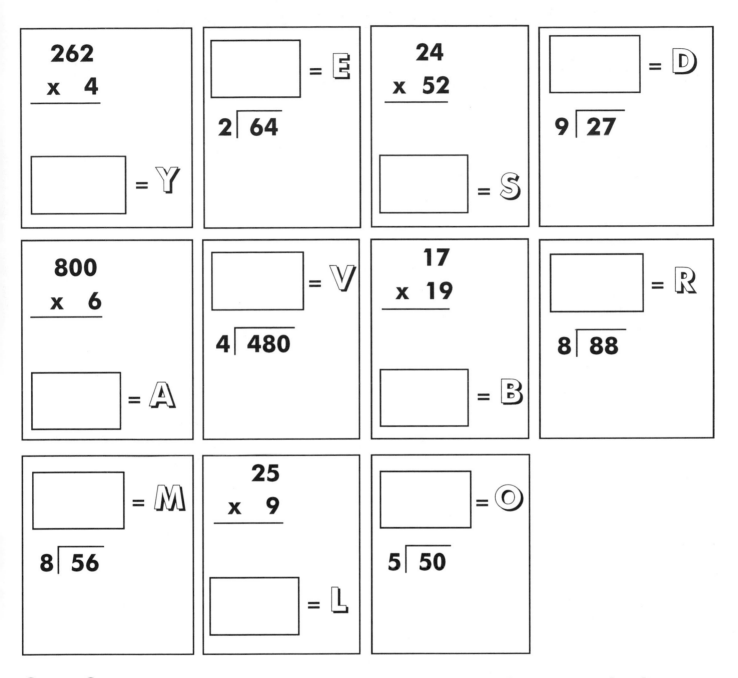

262
x 4

[   ] = Y

[   ] = E
2 ⟌ 64

24
x 52

[   ] = S

[   ] = D
9 ⟌ 27

800
x 6

[   ] = A

[   ] = V
4 ⟌ 480

17
x 19

[   ] = B

[   ] = R
8 ⟌ 88

[   ] = M
8 ⟌ 56

25
x 9

[   ] = L

[   ] = O
5 ⟌ 50

Step 2: To read the message, write the correct letter on the line.

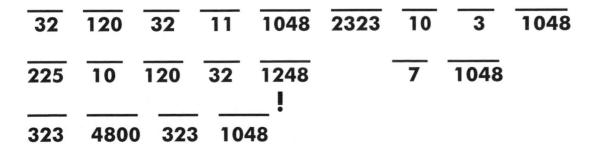

‾32‾ ‾120‾ ‾32‾ ‾11‾ ‾1048‾ ‾2323‾ ‾10‾ ‾3‾ ‾1048‾

‾225‾ ‾10‾ ‾120‾ ‾32‾ ‾1248‾   ‾7‾ ‾1048‾

‾___‾ ‾___‾ ‾___‾ ‾___‾ !
323   4800   323   1048

Quotation Marks
"Everybody Loves My Baby"

Directions: Put quotation marks around the words of the speaker.

Example: Millie said, "Charlie, should I bob my hair?"

1. No, said Charlie. What is his record?

2. Yeah, said Millie sarcastically.

3. Father, said Millie, when are you going to catch up with 1924?

4. Good night, father, said Millie.

5. Millie's father shook his head and said, Young people! They're runnin' wild.

6. Charlie said, It's just a song.

7. Oh my goodness, said father. What would your mother say?

8. Guess what we got today? asked Charlie.

Directions: Identify one character from the story and complete the chart below.

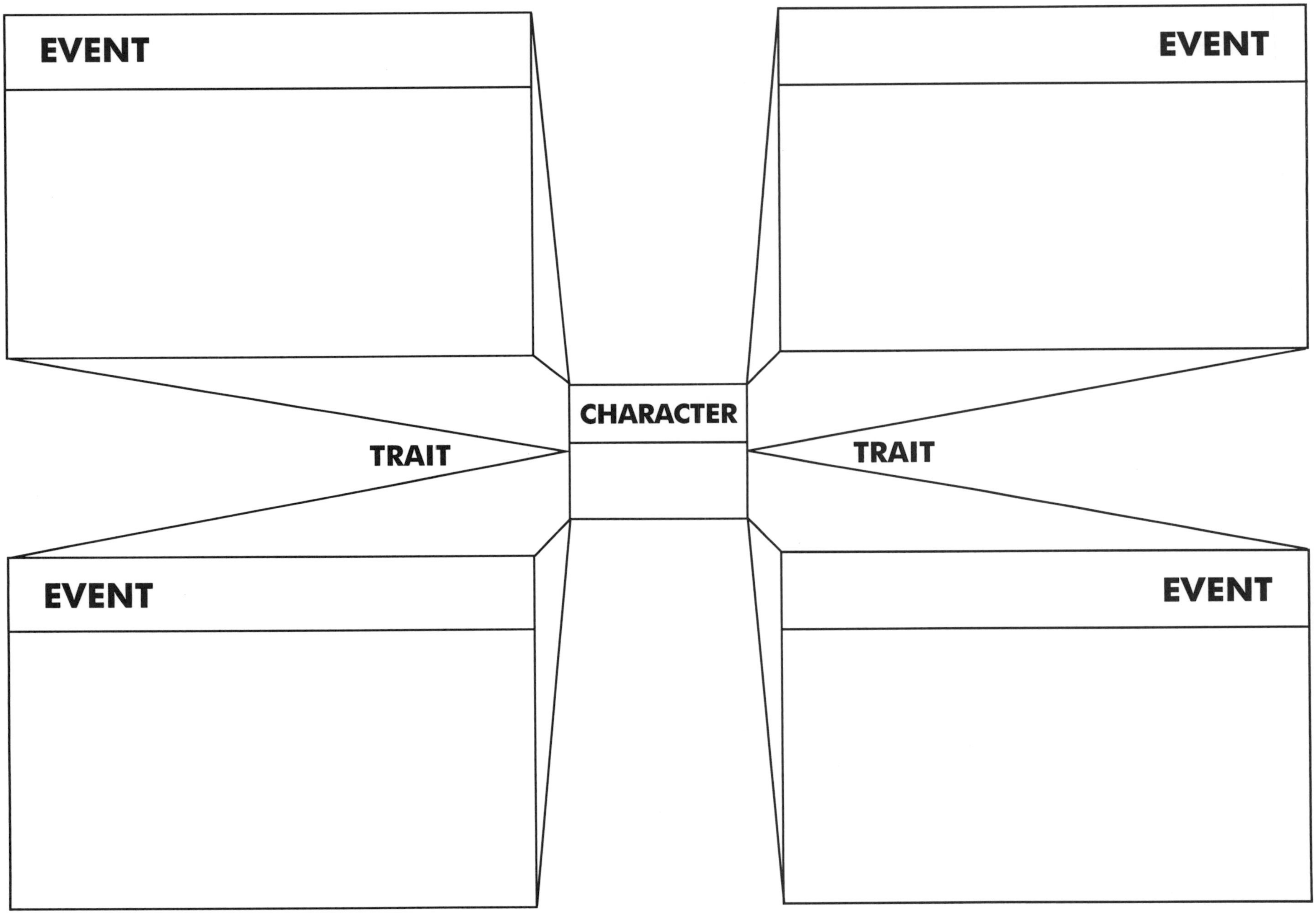

EVENT		EVENT
	CHARACTER	
	TRAIT	
EVENT		EVENT

Overview
"Tain't What You Do"

This story features an explanation of an arranger's job and many of the terms associated with conducting an orchestra. The integrated curriculum is based on <u>fourth</u> grade curricular concepts.*

Themes:
The themes of this story center on these concepts:
- Identifying the main idea and supporting details
- Geometry concepts
- Map skills - longitude and latitude
- Developing comprehensive paragraphs
- Understanding the scientific method
- Style of communication based on an audience

Integration of Themes:
The following connections can be made between the curricular concepts and the story line:

- The story focuses on the arranger's job which is to coordinate various instruments into a cohesive, well blended, piece of music. This requires the ability to organize multiple instruments into one final production. Application of this concept to the curriculum finds similarities in identifying main idea and paragraph development. Both skills require the student to arrange pieces of information into comprehensive paragraphs. They integrate ideas in order to develop a topic sentence (main idea), several supporting details and a conclusion, which are similar features to the job of an arranger.

- Another major theme throughout this story is how the combination of various instruments effects the final product. The scientific method requires students to integrate several pieces of information to arrive at a final conclusion. Map skills visually represent the integration that is apparent through studying the concepts of longitude and latitude. These concepts can be related to various game plays as the students study various sports. Development of the inter-relatedness of various positions and their contribution to the game provide students with an opportunity to experience this concept of integration first hand.

* For students who do not possess the reading skills necessary to read the story the teacher, or one of the students should read the story and tell it to them. Next, teach the vocabulary of the story and read the story aloud to the students who lack the reading skills necessary to read it themselves.

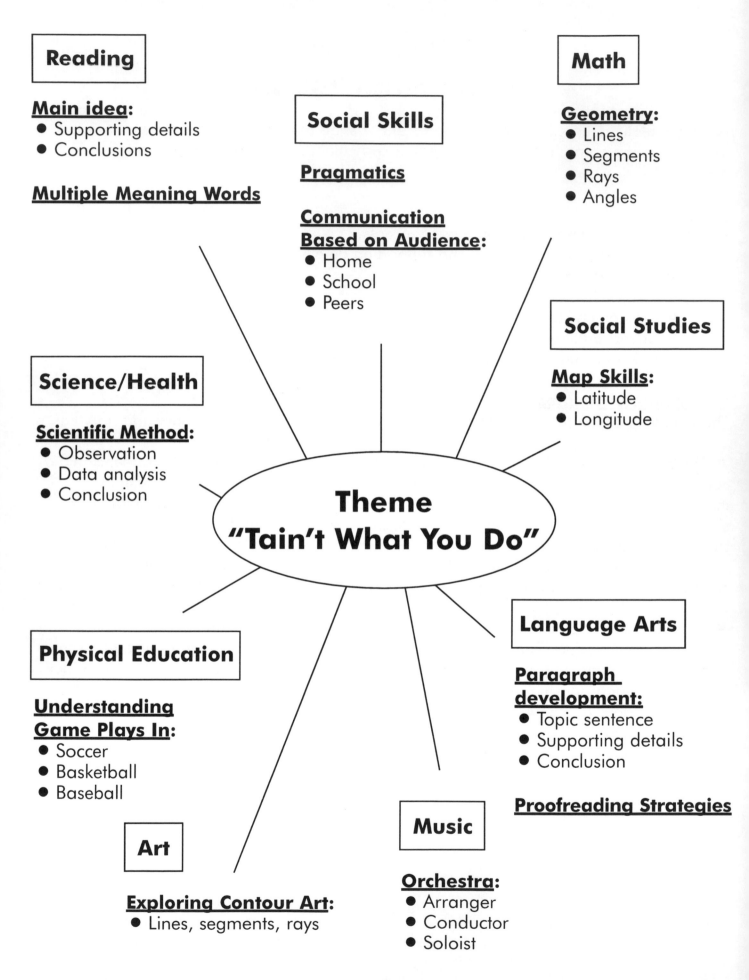

Reading

Main idea:
- Supporting details
- Conclusions

Multiple Meaning Words

Social Skills

Pragmatics

**Communication
Based on Audience:**
- Home
- School
- Peers

Math

Geometry:
- Lines
- Segments
- Rays
- Angles

Social Studies

Map Skills:
- Latitude
- Longitude

Science/Health

Scientific Method:
- Observation
- Data analysis
- Conclusion

Theme "Tain't What You Do"

Language Arts

Paragraph development:
- Topic sentence
- Supporting details
- Conclusion

Proofreading Strategies

Physical Education

Understanding Game Plays In:
- Soccer
- Basketball
- Baseball

Art

Exploring Contour Art:
- Lines, segments, rays

Music

Orchestra:
- Arranger
- Conductor
- Soloist

"Tain't What You Do"

The music and lyrics of "It Ain't What You Do, It's the Way That You Do It" were written by African-American trumpet player, singer, composer and arranger Sy Oliver. It was 1939 and Oliver was working in Jimmie Lunceford's Big Band with his friend, trombonist, Trummy Young. Young had improvised a beautiful trombone solo during one of the band's nite-club dates. Afterwards, Oliver said, "Trummy, that solo was fine. What was it you did in the last two bars?"

Trummy Young smiled and said, "Tain't what you do - it's the way that you do it," and the two of them playfully began to chant the statement back and forth. They started laughing and Oliver said, "Hey, Trummy, we could turn this into a song." So they did.

That year, the song was recorded by the Jimmy Lunceford band. Sy Oliver sang the vocals. The song, a big hit, was then recorded by a twenty-one year old woman. She became one of the greatest jazz singers in history - her name was Ella Fitzgerald.

Sy Oliver, the composer of "Tain't What You Do . . .," was one of our greatest swing band arrangers. An arranger's job is to write out the parts for the various musical instruments in the band so everyone knows what to play and when to play it. What he writes is called an "orchestration" or a "score." Small jazz groups don't necessarily need an arranger, they can make up music as they go along. It is necessary for Big Bands (with 12–30 instruments) to have an arranger to help the musicians start together, stay together and stop together.

Big Band arranging is a very complicated job. The arranger needs to know a lot about every instrument. He has to know how to blend different instruments to create different kinds of sounds. He has to know how to write a score that shows what every musical instrument is playing from the beginning to the end of the music.

Though the arranger is often not even seen by audiences, it is he who creates the one-of-a-kind sound of any first-rate Big Band. In many ways, the arranger is the most important member of the Big Band, even more important than the leader. Sy Oliver arranged for two of the swing era's greatest bands-the Jimmie Lunceford band and the Tommy Dorsey band. Every year from 1941 to 1945, *Downbeat Magazine* voted Sy Oliver America's greatest arranger.

A jazz fan once asked Oliver why his arrangements were always so exciting. Guess what his answer was? "It ain't what you do, it's the way that you do it!"

*   *   *   *   *

On the *Jazzing Up Instruction* CD, after the vocal part of "It Ain't What You Do . . .", pianist Dotty Tim plays a piano solo. In her solo, she plays two "quotes." A quote, in jazz, is a very short piece of another song played as part of the solo. Pianist Count Basie sometimes used quotes for humorous effect in an occasional solo. He injected little bits of songs like "Pop Goes the Weasel" or "Lazy Mary, Will You Get Up?" (See if you can find any other quotes on the *Jazzing Up Instruction* CD).

The first quote in "Tain't What You Do . . ." is used at the beginning of Dotty Tim's solo. She plays the opening two measures (eight beats) of Duke Ellington's, "I Let a Song Go Out of My Heart." Listen to this quote and when it appears, sing along with it.

The second quote, which comes a little later, is also from a Duke Ellington song. This one is called "Things Ain't What They Used to Be." The words, "You gotta get up this morning" fit this quote. Listen to the CD and sing the quote once you've found it.

Song Lyrics
"Tain't What You Do"

(A) (3 times)   Tain't what you do it's the way that
                 you do it
                 that's what gets results

                 Tain't what you say it's the way that
                 you say it
                 that's what gets results

(B)   You gotta try hard - don't give up
                 You gotta work hard - that's the stuff

(A)   Tain't what you do it's the way that
                 you do it
                 that's what gets results

                 Tain't what you say it's the way that
                 you say it
                 that's what gets results

Comprehension
"Tain't What You Do"

1. What does the song title, "Tain't What You Do, It's The Way That You Do It" mean?

2. Why is the arranger's job important to the orchestra?

3. How does a "quote" in jazz differ from a quote in a story?

4. Who is Ella Fitzgerald?

Vocabulary
"Tain't What You Do"

<u>Directions</u>: Define the following words.

1. orchestration -

2. score -

3. chant -

4. vocal -

5. arranger -

6. conductor -

7. measure -

8. tune -

"Tain't What You Do"

Directions: For each word below, define __two__ different meanings.

1. score _____

_____

2. tune _____

_____

3. measure _____

_____

4. arranger _____

_____

5. ring _____

_____

6. strike _____

_____

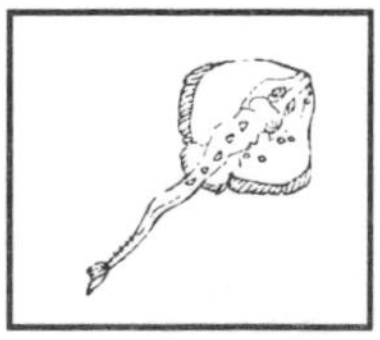

7. ray _____

_____

8. watch _____

_____

Main Idea:

Big Band arranging is a very complicated job. The arranger needs to know a lot about every instrument. He has to know how to blend different instruments to create different kinds of sounds. He has to know how to write a score that shows what every musical instrument is playing from the beginning to the end of the music.

Directions:

Read about Big Band arranging. Answer the questions below.

1. The main idea is:

    _____ Big Band arranging is a hard job.

    _____ The arranger needs to know how to write a score.

2. What are the two things the arranger needs to know?

    a. _____

    _____

    b. _____

    _____

3. How many instruments are usually in a big band?

_____

Geometry:
Lines, Segments, Rays, & Angles

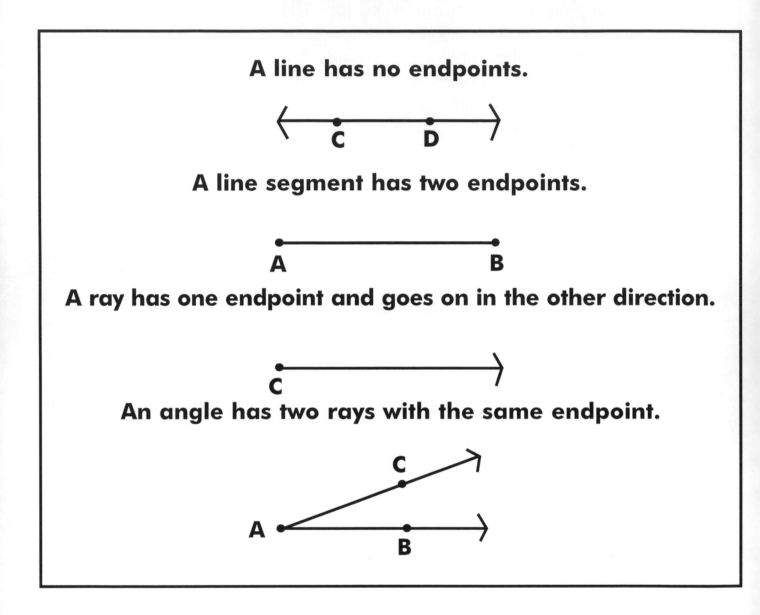

A line has no endpoints.

C   D

A line segment has two endpoints.

A   B

A ray has one endpoint and goes on in the other direction.

C

An angle has two rays with the same endpoint.

C

A   B

Directions: Identify each of the following as a line, line segment, ray or angle.

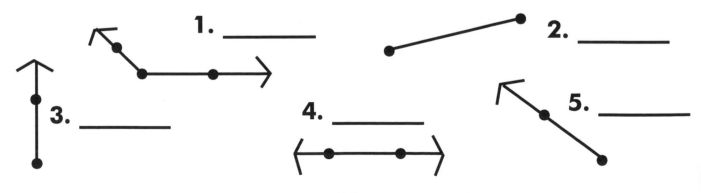

1. _____

2. _____

3. _____

4. _____

5. _____

92

Overview
"It Don't Mean A Thing"

This story chronicles the life of Duke Ellington and the creation of the Swing Era. The integrated curriculum framework is based on <u>fifth</u> grade curricular concepts.*

Themes:

The themes of this story center around these concepts:

- Sequencing
- Personal appearance/hygiene
- Developing healthy bodies
- Writing to persuade and compliment
- Fractions
- 1930's time period

Integration of Themes:

The following connection can be made between curricular concepts and the story line:

- The story provides a timeline of the creation of the Swing Era. This relates well to the development of story lines and outlines which reinforces the ability to sequence events and time. Recipes also follow a sequence of adding ingredients with steps necessary for the dessert to turn out properly.

- The story describes Duke Ellington as a snappy dresser and the importance of making a good appearance. Duke was known for complimenting women. These two characteristics highlight the significance of personal appearance, good grooming habits and the social skill of offering compliments to others.

- Math concepts include fractions, which are inherent in reading musical notes and measuring ingredients in recipes. Students experience how fractions are integrated throughout various subjects and necessary life skills.

- The Swing Era provides an opportunity to study famous Black Americans, learn about inflation and the effects it has on society and look at The Cotton Club in Harlem. Students integrate this with their knowledge of time lines and progression of events.

- Duke Ellington's complimentary style provides an opportunity for students to practice writing skills, in form of thank you notes and complimentary praise. This reinforces the development of proper etiquette and pro-social skills.

• The cultural arts provide the students with practice in reading musical notes (fractions) and a historical perspective on fashion, then and now. Students will compare and contrast current trends with those of the 1930's.

• Physical education focuses on the development of healthy bodies required to perform the various dances of the 1930's. Students can enjoy the opportunity to learn some of the dances performed during the Swing Era and the physical conditioning required to do so. Integration of this concept with good hygiene promotes the development of health habits.

• Science provides an opportunity to integrate several concepts together: healthy bodies, hygiene, physical conditioning and nutrition. Students develop the ability to see the inter-connectedness with other content areas and the relevance in their daily lives.

* For students who do not possess the reading skills necessary to read the story the teacher, or one of the students should read the story and tell it to them. Next, teach the vocabulary of the story and read the story aloud to the students who lack the reading skills necessary to read it themselves.

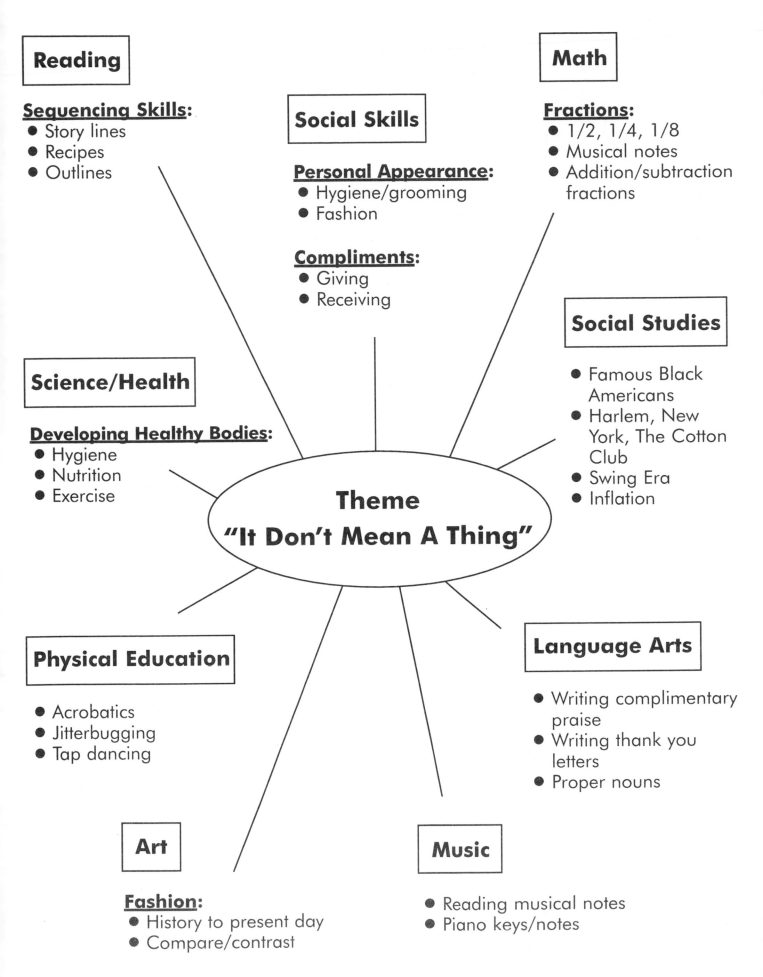

Reading

Sequencing Skills:
- Story lines
- Recipes
- Outlines

Social Skills

Personal Appearance:
- Hygiene/grooming
- Fashion

Compliments:
- Giving
- Receiving

Math

Fractions:
- 1/2, 1/4, 1/8
- Musical notes
- Addition/subtraction fractions

Science/Health

Developing Healthy Bodies:
- Hygiene
- Nutrition
- Exercise

Social Studies
- Famous Black Americans
- Harlem, New York, The Cotton Club
- Swing Era
- Inflation

Theme
"It Don't Mean A Thing"

Physical Education
- Acrobatics
- Jitterbugging
- Tap dancing

Language Arts
- Writing complimentary praise
- Writing thank you letters
- Proper nouns

Art

Fashion:
- History to present day
- Compare/contrast

Music
- Reading musical notes
- Piano keys/notes

"It Don't Mean A Thing"

In America, the time period from 1930 to 1950 is often called the "Swing Era." The most popular <u>sound</u> of this period was Big Band music, the perfect background for the popular style of dance called "jitterbugging." Good jitterbugs had to be very athletic because they would lift one another off the dance floor and jump over each other. Jitterbugging was a little like acrobatics done to music.

In 1932, Duke Ellington wrote a song that was very popular with people who liked to jitterbug. It was called, "It Don't Mean A Thing If It Ain't Got That Swing." After Ellington wrote that song, people started calling Big Band music "swing" and the Swing Era had begun.

America had many jobless people during the 1930's, so they had little money, but, for a nickel, they could play some swing music at the local soda shop and jitterbug to their heart's content. A popular saying during these years was, "Swing is king!"

Duke Ellington may not have been the inventor of swing music, but his band was one of the best and one of the most popular. Who knows what the time between 1930 and 1950 would have been called if Duke Ellington's song hadn't give the era a name? Ellington was proud of his music's popularity, but this popularity didn't suddenly happen. It was the result of years of hard work.

*   *   *   *   *

Edward Kennedy "Duke" Ellington was born in Washington, D.C. in 1889. When he was seven, he began studying piano, but he had such a good <u>musical ear</u> that he often learned his music by listening to his teacher play instead of reading his music. As a result, Duke didn't read music very well.

When Duke was 17, he became serious about music, and he auditioned for a job playing piano in a dance band in Washington, D.C. (By this time, Duke had worked hard to improve his music reading skills). He won the audition and his playing soon caught people's attention.

Duke was not only concerned about playing well, but also with looking good. A very <u>snappy dresser</u>, his clothes fit "<u>like a glove</u>" and were color coordinated. Women loved Duke because he said things that made them feel special. To a female fan he said, "I can tell you're an angel; I can see the reflection of your halo shining on the ceiling." Another complement he often used was, "My, but you make that dress look lovely!" At this time, when Duke played piano, he would lift his hands dramatically whenever he finished playing a musical passage. This is when people started calling him "The Duke," because he acted like royalty and people (women especially) began treating him that way.

Soon Duke formed his own band, which he called the "Washingtonians." When Duke was 24, he traveled to New York City to try playing in the big time. After playing in a cabaret called the Kentucky Club, Duke Ellington formed a new band with 12 players to play at the biggest club in Harlem - The Cotton Club. Soon he was recording. Before he was 30 years old, the Duke's band was sent to Hollywood to be featured in films.

In 1998, when the Smithsonian Museum in Washington, D.C., honored America's four greatest swing bands, they chose Duke Ellington's band <u>number one</u>. He made over 2,000 recordings over a 50-year period. Many of the songs he recorded were best sellers - like "Sophisticated Lady," "Mood Indigo," "Take the 'A' Train," and "Satin Doll." Duke Ellington dressed well, spoke well, wrote music still popular 70 years after it was first heard. He left behind millions of devoted fans. Duke was proud of his black heritage and this partial list of Ellington compositions shows that pride:

- "Mood Indigo"
- "Black and Tan Fantasy"
- "Black Butterfly"
- "Creole Rhapsody"
- "Harlem Air Shaft"
- "Harmony in Harlem"
- "Afro-Bossa"
- "Black, Brown and Beige"

- "Black Beauty"
- "Brown-skin Gal in the Calico Gown"
- "Ebony Rhapsody"
- "Echoes of Harlem"
- "Portrait of Louis Armstrong"
- "Harlem"
- "Symphony in Black"
- "What Color is Love?"

All of these Duke Ellington compositions have a beat that makes you tap your toes and snap your fingers. The Ellington compositions have to make you do that because, as Duke said, "It don't mean a thing if it ain't got that swing!"

Song Lyrics
"It Don't Mean A Thing"

(A) It don't mean a thing if it ain't
     got that swing   Do-wa, Do-wa, Do-wa,
     Do-wa, Do-wa, Do-wa, Do-wa, Do-wa

(A) It don't mean a thing all you got
     to do is sing   Do-wa, Do-wa, Do-wa,
     Do-wa, Do-wa, Do-wa, Do-wa, Do-wa

(B) It makes no difference if it's cool or hot
     You gotta give that rhythm everything
     you got

(A) It don't mean a thing if it ain't
     got that swing   Do-wa, Do-wa, Do-wa,
     Do-wa, Do-wa, Do-wa, Do-wa, Do-wa

Comprehension
"It Don't Mean A Thing"

1. Compare jobless people during the 1930's to the homeless today.

2. How did Duke compensate for his poor music reading skills and what impact did that have on his future?

3. How did Duke's personality and style influence his success? What implications could it have on your future success?

4. The period between 1930 to 1950 is known as the "Swing Era." What do you think would characterize the 1990's?

5. How did inflation effect the "Swing Era" and what effect does it have on us

Vocabulary
"It Don't Mean A Thing"

<u>Directions</u>: Define the following words.

1. Jitterbugging -

2. heritage -

3. auditioned -

4. cabaret -

5. reflection -

6. acrobatics -

7. compositions -

8. coordinated -

Pavlova
"It Don't Mean A Thing"

Ingredients:
(Serves 12)

- **1/2cup cool fresh egg whites (approximately 4 eggs)**
- **pinch of salt**
- **1/2 teaspoon vanilla**
- **1/2 teaspoon cream of tartar**
- **1 cup granulated sugar**
- **4 kiwis or 12-14 strawberries**
- **1 cup whipped topping**

1. Preheat the oven to 250 degrees.

2. In a mixing bowl put the 4 egg whites, salt, 1/2 teaspoon of vanilla and 1/2 teaspoon of cream of tarter. To create a meringue, blend the egg whites, salt, vanilla, and cream of tartar for approximately four minutes with a mixer.

3. After about 2 minutes, gradually add one cup of sugar. Beat until stiff peaks form.

4. Spoon a heaping tablespoon of meringue onto a greased baking sheet. Hollow the middle of the meringue with the back of a spoon.

5. Bake for 1 & 1/2 hours at 250 degrees.

6. Turn off the heat and leave the meringues in the oven for ten minutes with the door open.

7. Meanwhile, peel and slice the kiwis or strawberries.

8. Layer kiwi or strawberry slices on the cooled shell and top with whipped topping.

Pavlova

"It Don't Mean A Thing"

Directions: Number the steps in order from 1 to 8 for making Pavlova.

_____ Bake for 1 & 1/2 hours at 250 degrees.

_____ Blend the egg whites, salt, vanilla, and cream of tartar for about four minutes with a mixer.

_____ Peel and slice the kiwi or strawberries.

_____ Spoon meringue onto a greased baking sheet. Hollow the middle of the meringue with the back of a spoon.

_____ Turn off heat. Leave the meringues in the oven for ten minutes with the door open.

_____ Gradually add one cup of sugar. Beat until stiff peaks form.

_____ Layer kiwi or strawberry slices on cooled shell. Top with whipped topping.

_____ Preheat the oven to 250 degrees.

Step 2: Highlight the fractions on the recipe.

Capital Letters in Names, Titles, and Places
"It Don't Mean A Thing"

Elvis Presley   **"Frosty the Snowman"**   **Mexico**

Rules:
- The first letter of a person's first, middle, and last name is <u>always</u> capitalized.
- Capitalize the first and last name of a title and all other words except short prepositions.
- <u>All</u> names of places are capitalized.

Directions: Capitalize the proper nouns in each sentence.

1. In america, the time period between 1930 to 1950 is often called the "swing era."

2. Duke ellington wrote a song that was very popular with people who liked to jitter-bug.

3. Edward kennedy "duke" ellington was born in washington, d.c.

4. The smithsonian museum in washington, d.c. honored america's four greatest swing bands.

5. Duke ellington wrote the song "sophisticated lady."

6. The biggest club in harlem was called the cotton club.

7. George simon wrote the book the big bands.

8. Black butterfly is a song written by duke ellington.

Directions:

Draw a comic strip showing how to **give** a compliment.

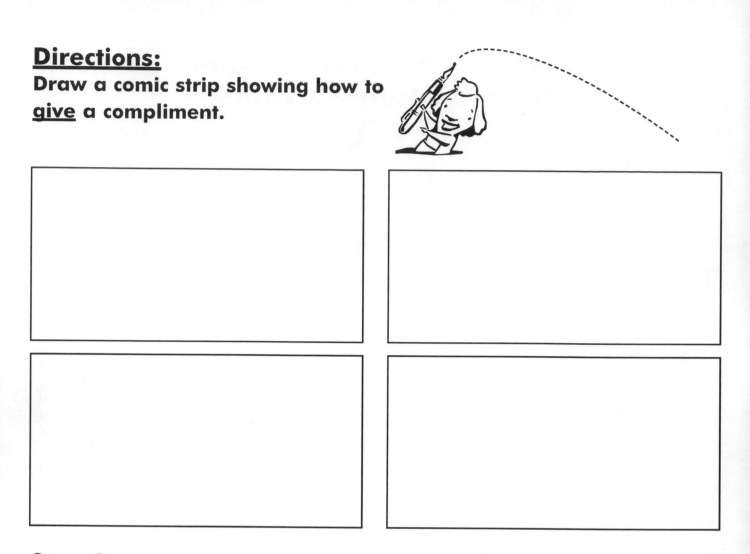

Step 2: Draw a comic strip showing how to **receive** a compliment.

Overview
"The Jazz Men"

This story chronicles the life of Louis Armstrong and how he became known as the "King of Jazz." The integrated curriculum is based on <u>fifth</u> grade curricular concepts.*

Themes:
The themes of this story center on these concepts:
- Character development
- Positive role models/attributes
- New Orleans/Mardi Gras
- Respiratory system
- Charting/graphing
- Abstract language

Integration of Themes:
Louis Armstrong's life serves as a role model for students. They gain an understanding of how he persevered through difficult times to become famous.

- The character traits that Louis Armstrong portrayed gives students an understanding of how they can be successful even if they go through some tough times in life. A positive attitude assists them in achieving goals and overcoming hurdles along the way.

- Louis' unique way of signing his letters made a mark for himself in life. Students can practice this skill while they reinforce their letter writing and song lyric skills. Integration of cultural arts can assist students with developing their own "mark" or flair for writing.

- The story describes Louis Armstrong's ability to play the trumpet, yet he needed to develop his lung capacity to hit the notes. Students can have fun determining their lung capacity, estimating how much lung capacity is needed to play various instruments and graph their findings.

- Studying New Orleans paves the way to the celebration of Mardi Gras. Students can compare/contrast Mardi Gras to holidays they share and the cultural diversity that exists. Creation of Mardi Gras masks is a fun project the students will enjoy making and wearing during Mardi Gras. This activity will assist the students in integrating all skills introduced during this unit.

* For students who do not possess the reading skills necessary to read the story the teacher, or one of the students should read the story and tell it to them. Next, teach the vocabulary of the story and read the story aloud to the students who lack the reading skills necessary to read it themselves.

Reading
- Character development
- Story timeline

Social Skills
- Positive attributes
- Gratitude
- Role models

Math

Charts/Graphs:
- Locating information
- Creating charts/graphs

Measuring Distance:
- Using various instruments
- Map legend

Science/Health

Respiratory System:
- Breath monitor
- Lungs

Social Studies

Study of New Orleans:
- Map skills
- Mardi Gras celebration

Theme "The Jazz Men"

Physical Education

Cardiovascular Exercise:
- Increasing breathing and endurance
- Recording exercise program

Language Arts
- Abstract language idioms
- Writing a friendly letter
- Writing song lyrics

Art
- Mardi Gras masks
- New Orleans style art

Music
- History of jazz
- Trumpet
- Other songs by Louis Armstrong

"The Jazz Men"

When Louis Armstrong was a little boy in New Orleans, he heard an old man on the street corner singing a song about a sick woman who was rushed to the hospital. When her husband arrived at the hospital, he found her lying on a long, white table and cried, "There'll never be another like her! Lord, there'll never be another for me!" Louis Armstrong never forgot that song, and in 1948, he recorded it, under the title, "St. James Infirmary Blues," playing trumpet and singing the song. It was the only sad song Louis Armstrong ever recorded, and it became one of his biggest selling recordings.

(On our CD, the words "I went down to St. James Infirmary" have been changed to "I went down to see the Jazz Man." The new words tell you about two great Jazz Men from New Orleans: Louis Armstrong and Sidney Bechet).

Louis was a cheerful boy. What his childhood friends remembered about him was that it was so easy to get him to laugh and that, more times than not, he had a smile on his face. He also loved to make other people laugh. All his life, Louis loved the food he'd eaten as a child in New Orleans. Instead of signing his letters "Sincerely yours," he'd often sign them "Red Beans and Ricely Yours."

In 1913, when Louis was twelve years old, he celebrated New Year's Eve by firing a pistol into the air at midnight. The neighbors called the police. Louis was arrested and after his trial was sent to the Colored Waif's Home where the music teacher, Peter Davis, taught him to play the trumpet. Over the next few years, Louis became one of the best trumpet players in New Orleans. Louis himself said that by the time he was 17, "I could read music very well . . . I could blow harder and longer without getting tired." A musician who knew Louis said, "High C is a hard note for any trumpet player to hit, but when Louis was at his peak, he would hit high C's like they were tennis balls."

At 17, Louis was playing lead trumpet with the Fate Marable band on the paddlewheeler excursion boat called the Dixie Belle. The boat would travel the Mississippi River from New Orleans, Louisiana to St. Louis, Missouri and back again. Soon people from other parts of the country were talking about the great young trumpet player, Louis Armstrong. In those days, Louis was very generous with his money. He would treat his friends to tickets at the silent movie shows. He sometimes paid to get his fellow musicians' instruments out of pawn shops so they could keep their jobs on the riverboat. As a result, Louis was usually broke. That changed later. By the late 1930's, Louis Armstrong would become one of the highest paid musicians in the world.

As Louis' fame grew, he moved to Chicago where he played in night clubs. From Chicago, Louis moved to New York City where he formed his own band and recorded his music. In February, 1934, the readers and staff of *Esquire Magazine* voted Louis Armstrong the greatest jazz trumpet player in America and called him the "King of Jazz."

Louis was a little embarrassed by all this adulation. He just kept on playing and singing and recording best selling songs like "On the Sunny Side of the Street," "Mack the Knife" and "Hello Dolly." He recorded "St. James Infirmary Blues" with the great jazz pianist Earl "Fatha" Hines forty years after he'd first heard it on the streets of New Orleans. Today, that city boasts an eight-foot-high bronze statue of Louis Armstrong. New York, the city Louis moved to, dedicated a museum to his reign as the "King of Jazz."

Song Lyrics
"The Jazz Men"

I went to see the jazz man
and hear him play his song
and when the blues surround me
I hear that Melody

We all now Louis Armstrong
he came from New Orleans
he sang and played the trumpet
and traveled 'round the world

Sidney play with Louis the
sax and clarinet
One day he moved to Paris
and wrote this melody

So don't forget the music
that came from Basin Street

It grew from many cultures
and spread throughout the land

Comprehension
"The Jazz Men"

1. Where was Louis born and how did this influence his vocation in life?

2. What event occurred in 1913? What impact did it have on Louis's life?

3. How did Louis's music career begin?

4. Describe the changes that occurred in Louis's musical career.

5. Develop a character profile of Louis.

Vocabulary
"The Jazz Men"

Directions: Define the following words.

1. excursion -

2. travel -

3. generous -

4. instrument -

5. pawn -

6. adulation -

7. boast -

8. arrested -

Compound Words
"The Jazz Men"

Directions: Find the compound words that describe the picture in the word search below.

```
A I R P L A N E T B O R P A R P A R Y
M O O R S S A L C O S X U P A M N H L
I D P S K U H J H R U Y T I T Y I V F
D X E S B R I K J E N E W S P A P E R
N A M L I A M Y M L S M L N M L N I E
I O L O G N O S S D H K E I A I V X T
G Y D A N X X M P L I P L G P E G P T
H R P L A Y G R O U N D A H R S H A U
T I A I H V I X E V E E V B E V T E B
D S E V E N T E E N P T O G M K X Q Y
N F P J E S Q M R E U A J J R J P Z I
R L A V U Y S N U E T A O C N I A R E
Y A Q P F I A A A Q B L I C J D D H P
W Y C E Z M M R M X A K P V F G W I N
S I X W N O N B D S C U A B Z M E J K
```

Directions: Illustrate the idioms below.

Example: Earl couldn't carry a tune.

1. It's going in one ear and out the other.

2. Andy put his foot in his mouth.

3. Louis has a frog in his throat.

4. Ella has butterflies in her stomach.

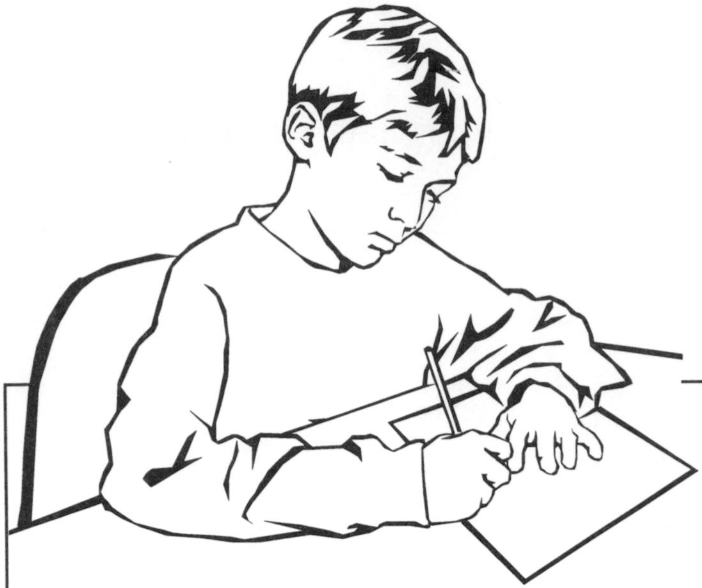

<u>Directions</u>:
Complete the friendly letter to Louis Armstrong. Create a unique closing of your own.

____

______________________,

I think your closing, "Red Beans and Ricely Yours," is . . .

____

____

____

____

____

____

____

____

Bibliography

Allen, Frederick Lewis. The Big Change 1900–1950 (New York: Harper and Row, 1952).

American Education Publishing, Comprehensive Curriculum of Basic Skills - Grade 1, (Ohio: 1993).

American Education Publishing, Comprehensive Curriculum of Basic Skills - Grade 2, (Ohio: 1993).

American Education Publishing, Comprehensive Curriculum of Basic Skills - Grade 4, (Ohio, 1993).

American Heritage (Special Issue, the 1920s), (August 1965, Volume XVI, number 5).

Armstrong, Louis. Swing that Music (New York: Longmans and Green, 1936).

Beirle, Marlene and Lynes, Teri. Book Cooks: Literature Based Classroom Cooking (California: Creative Teaching Press, Inc., 1992).

Brown, Ron and Nancy. Use Music To Teach! (California: 1991).

Bryan, Sandra L. and Sprague, Marsha M. Educating the Spirit for Beauty. (Vol. 2, Number 4, December 1998/January 1999).

Butterworth, W. E. Hi-fi - From Edison's Phonograph to Quadraphonic Sound (New York: Four Winds Press, 1977).

Chipongian, Lisa. What is "Brain-Based Learning?" (California, 1999).

Clarke, Donald. The Rise and Fall of Popular Music (New York: St. Martins Press, 1995).

Collier, James Lincoln. Benny Goodman and the Swing Era (New York: Oxford University Press, 1989).

Copland, Aaron. Music and Imagination (Boston: Harvard University Press, 1952).

Crow, Bill. Jazz Anecdotes (Oxford, England: Oxford University Press, 1990).

Davis, Francis. The History of the Blues (New York: Hyperion Publishers, 1995).

Editor, Ernest R. May. The Life History of the United States (Volume 10: 1917–1932) (New York: Time-Life Books, 1974).

Editors, Hentoff, Nat and McCarthy, Albert J., Jazz-New Perspectives on the History of Jazz by Twelve of the World's Foremost Jazz Critics and Scholars (New York: Rhinehart and Company, 1959) (Article cited: New Orleans and Traditions in Jazz, Charles Edward Smith).

Ewen, David. Men of Popular Music (New York: Ziff-Davis Publishing, 1944).

Ferris, William. Blues from the Delta (New York: Doubleday, 1978).

Garcia, Russel. The Professional Arranger Composer (Hollywood: Criterion Music Corporation, 1954).

Gelatt, Roland. The Fabulous Phonograph (New York: MacMillan, 1977).

Gourse, Leslie. The Ella Fitzgerald Companion (New York: Schirmer Books, 1998).

Handy, W.C. Father of the Blues (New York: Macmillan, 1941).

Hanson, E. Simon, A New Approach to Learning: The Theory of Multiple Intelligences. (California, 1999).

Hardy, Phil and Dave Laing. The DaCapo Companion to the 20th Century Popular Music (New York: DaCapo Press, 1995).

Jensen, Eric. Arts with the Brain in Mind (Virginia: ASCD, 2001).

Jensen, Eric, Brain Compatible Strategies (San Diego: ASCD, 1997).

Jensen, Eric, Teaching with the Brain in Mind (San Diego: ASCD, 1998).

Jourdan, Robert. Music, The Brain and Ecstasy. (New York: William Morrow and Company, 1997).

Kane, Henry. How to Write a Song (Interviews with the Great Popular Song Writers) (New York: The MacMillan Company, 1962).

Kovalik, Susan and Olsen, Karen. ITI: THE MODEL Integrated Thematic Instruction (Washington: Books for Educators, 1994).

Lickona, Thomas, Educating for Character: How our Schools Can Teach Respect and Responsibility (New York: Bantam Books, 1991).

Linton, Chiswick, Milestones of Jazz (Surrey, England: CLB International, 1997).

Lissauer, Robert. Lissauer's Encyclopedia of Popular Music in America (1888 to the Present) (New York: Facts on File, 1996).

Lissauer, Robert. Lissauer's Encyclopedia of Popular Music - 1888 to 1996 (New York: Facts on File Books, 1996).

Millard, Andre. America on Record - A History of Recorded Sound (Cambridge, England: Cambridge University Press, 1995).

Montgomery, Elizabeth. <u>The Stories Behind Popular Songs</u> (New York: Dodd and Mead, 1958).

Merlis, Bob and Seay, Davin. <u>Heart and Soul (A Celebration of Black Music In America)</u> (New York: Stewart, Tabori and Chang, 1997).

Musselwhite, Caroline Ramsey. <u>Singing to learn: Using music to jump-start language, literacy and life!</u>

Schuller, Gunther. <u>The Swing Era</u> (Oxford, England: Oxford University Press, 1989).

Sousa, David A. <u>How the Brain Learns</u> (Virginia: National Association of Secondary School Principals, 1995).

Southern, Eileen. <u>The Music of Black Americans</u> (New York: W. W. Norton, 1971).

Sprenger, Marilee, <u>Learning and Memory - The Brain in Action</u> (Virginia: ASCD, 1999).

Studwell, William E. and Baldwin, Mark, <u>The Big Band Reader</u> (Binghamton, NY: The Haworth Press, 2000).

Tyler, Don. <u>Hit Parade 1920-1955</u> (New York: William Morrow, 1985).

Weinberger, N.M. <u>The Impact of the Arts on Learning.</u> (Volume VII, Issue 2, Spring, 2000).

Whitburn, Joel. <u>Pop Memories 1890–1954</u>. (Menamonee Falls, Wisconsin, 1986).

Wilder, Alex. <u>American Popular Song</u> (Oxford, England: Oxford University Press, 1972).

Wolfinger, Donna M. and Stockward, James W. <u>Elementary Methods: An Integrated Curriculum</u> (New York: Longman, 1997).

Wood, Ean. <u>Born to Swing (the Story of the Big Bands)</u> (London: Santuary Publishing, Ltd., 1966).

Yopp, Hallie Kay. <u>Building a Powerful Reading Program.</u>

About The Children's Guild

The Children's Guild, a not-for-profit organization based in Baltimore, Maryland, is a national leader in special education. Using a philosophy called Transformation Education, The Guild brings together a unique educational program, stimulating environments, and an integrated approach to help children with emotional disabilities learn to become successful in life.

The Guild's commitment to children with special needs and innovative ways to educate them began in 1953. It was founded by Sadie Ginsberg, an internationally known children's advocate, Dr. Leo Kanner, the father of child psychiatry and the discoverer of childhood autism, and Dr. Matthew Debuskey, a prominent Baltimore pediatrician.

Today, The Children's Guild is one of the largest provider of special education day programs for emotionally disturbed children in the State of Maryland. The Guild operates three schools located in: Baltimore City, Anne Arundel and Prince George's counties.

The Guild's school programs accept boys and girls from first grade through high school. Its school programs are approved by the Maryland State Department of Education and licensed by the Maryland State Department of Health and Mental Hygiene. The Guild is accredited by the Council on Accreditation for Children and Families and its schools in Baltimore City and Anne Arundel County are accredited by the National Commission Accrediting Special Education Services.

In addition to its school programs, The Guild provides special programs and services for children and their families, including:

- The After-School Program for children with special needs (Baltimore City)
- Summer School for children with special needs (Baltimore City, Anne Arundel and Prince George's counties)
- High School (Baltimore City)
- School-to-Work Program for students ages 14 to 21 (Baltimore City)
- Preschool for children ages 3 to 5 with emotional disabilities (Baltimore City)
- Diagnostic and Evaluation Services (Anne Arundel County)
- Family Help Center, an outpatient clinic offering mental health services (Baltimore City)
- Therapeutic Group Homes for boys ages 12-18 (Baltimore City)

For more information, contact The Children's Guild at 1-800-510-0273 or 1-410-444-3800.

Website: www.childrensguild.org

Jazzing Up Instruction Credits

Authors

Kelly Spanoghe - Created the Teacher Workbook.

Kelly is the Director of Education at The Children's Guild's Annapolis, Maryland Campus and has been a special education teacher and an administrator of special education programs since 1982. She received her B.A. in Special Education from the University of Maryland and her M.A. and Ed.S. in Special Education from George Washington University.

Laura L. Peter - Assisted Kelly Spanoghe in creating the Teacher Worksheets.

Laura earned a B.A. in Special Education from the University of West Florida.

Bill Messenger - Researched and authored the 10 original stories of the musician's lives.

Bill is a teacher, composer, historian and lecturer at the Peabody Conservatory of Music and the originator of The Children's Guild Music program. He possesses a B.A. in Music from Towson University with emphasis on musical composition from the Peabody Institute and two master degrees from Johns Hopkins, one in Writing and one in English Literature. Bill has 200 published articles to his credit and has written music criticism for The Baltimore Sun, The Baltimore Magazine and The Baltimore News American.

Concept Designer

Andrew L. Ross - Created the concept of *Jazzing Up Instruction* and directed and produced this project.

Andy is President and CEO of The Children's Guild and has been involved in educating, managing and developing innovative programs to educate and resocialize special needs children for 35 years. He possesses a B.A. in Psychology from Thiel College and an M.A. and Ph.D. in Social Work from Case Western Reserve University. Andy has published numerous articles on treating children with emotional disturbance and led and authored a national study to prevent child abuse and neglect in institutions for disadvantaged children.